JEWELRY
MARKETING JOY

An Approachable Introduction
to Marketing Your Jewelry Brand

Laryssa Wirstiuk

Joy Joya LLC

Los Angeles, CA

Joy Joya LLC
PO Box 27411
Los Angeles, CA, 90027
www.joyjoya.com

Book Layout © 2017 BookDesignTemplates.com
Cover Design by Jordan Harris
Cover Photo by Alain Simic
Author Photo by Matthew Freund

Jewelry Marketing Joy / Laryssa Wirstiuk -- 1st ed.
ISBN 978-0-9858319-4-3

Special thanks to Jordan Harris, Cheryl and Matthew Freund, Alain Simic, Nan Lung Palmer, Charlotte Moo, and all the jewelry entrepreneurs focused on bringing more beauty and sparkle into the world.

Don't just create what
the market needs or wants.
Create what it would love.

HARRY BECKWITH

CONTENTS

What do baseball diamonds have in common with sparkling diamond jewelry? You've likely heard the phrase "If you build it, they will come", which is actually a misquote from the 1989 film Field of Dreams. In the film, Kevin Costner's character Ray hears a mysterious voice, which tells him, "If you build it, he will come." Ray interprets the message as a call to build a baseball diamond on his property, and he obeys. Once the baseball diamond is built, deceased baseball players emerge from the cornfields to play.

Whether they admit it to themselves or not, many jewelry entrepreneurs are like Ray. At some point in time, they hear a voice in their heads that tells them to start a jewelry business, either a brick-and-mortar store or an ecommerce shop. They may not consciously believe that running and sustaining a business will be as easy as simply building it, but they also don't necessarily have a solid business and marketing plan in place. Effectively, they're like Ray, believing that - as long as they build the storefront - the customers will come.

In some very rare cases, this approach may actually work. For example, a jewelry retailer may open in a town that's quickly developing but doesn't yet have a jewelry store. By default, the residents will likely patronize the store (if they're not already shopping online). However, with the advent of easy-to-implement ecommerce solutions like Shopify, literally anyone with an Internet connection and a credit card can set up shop. In October 2019, Shopify announced that it had surpassed one million merchants worldwide on the platform. The "If you build it, they will come" mentality simply doesn't serve today's jewelry business owner.

According to data from Grand View Research, Inc.,[1] the total global jewelry market is expected to reach a value of $480.5 billion U.S. dollars by 2025. In addition, a promising report from McKinsey states that the category has a "multifaceted future" and that the "Consumer appetite for jewelry...now appears more voracious than ever".[2] Branded jewelry especially is taking up more market share than ever before. The same McKinsey report predicted that branded jewelry would account for about 40% of the market in 2020, and the popularity of branded jewelry among consumers only continues to grow. The good news is that there's definitely a place in the market for your jewelry, as long as you can distin-

JEWELRY MARKETING JOY · iii

guish your brand from others and captivate consumer interest.

Marketing - especially when it complements your desirable jewelry products and attractive price points - is one of the best ways to generate brand awareness, but marketing also has so many subsets that most jewelry entrepreneurs struggle to prioritize their marketing efforts and piece together an effective marketing strategy.

To make matters even more complicated, today's consumers are savvier than ever before, and they have many options - not only when it comes to products but also sales channels. They can shop in store, through an ecommerce website, on an app, and even through a social media platform, depending on their mood and preferences. As a result, your jewelry brand must work hard to meet the customers where they are at any given time.

Understanding what marketing can help your jewelry brand achieve is the first step in moving forward toward growth. If you don't know what's possible, then you won't be able to leverage the best tools effectively. In this book, I'll demystify marketing, so you can start taking action by implementing the necessary steps yourself or hiring someone to do them for you.

Who will benefit from this book?

I wrote this book with independent jewelry entrepreneurs and their team members in mind. The information I share will be most useful for direct-to-consumer brands and traditional retailers that maintain an ecommerce presence or that use digital marketing to drive traffic to a brick-and-mortar store or other sales channel.

This book is not for you if you only maintain a brick-and-mortar store and do not plan to cultivate any type of digital presence, like a website or social media profiles. I won't be covering more traditional marketing methods like direct mail or print advertising, so you'll need to feel comfortable using digital platforms or hiring someone to navigate them for you.

I believe the ultimate purpose of marketing is to build lasting, meaningful relationships with customers, so if you're looking for a quick fix, this book is not for you. You'll need to be prepared to think of marketing as a long game. As a general rule, you should plan to engage in marketing for as long as you'd like to be running your business; the two go hand in hand. The work of building brand awareness, creating value, and forging bonds with your customers takes time and effort.

Whether you're building your marketing strategy for the first time, or you're refining your current marketing strategy, then you'll benefit from the insights in the coming pages. My goal is to help you lay an effective marketing foundation upon which you can build for many years to come. I'm excited to show you the way forward.

Who am I, and why should you listen to me?

When I tell people I'm the founder and creative director of a digital marketing agency that works exclusively with jewelry brands, most are amazed by the specificity of my work. Many are delighted that they've found someone who specializes in their niche and can speak the language of the industry. So how did I decide to focus on the jewelry industry in the first place, and how did my background get me to this point?

Basically, I'm obsessed with jewelry. When I was in college studying communications and writing, I would watch Jewelry Television (JTV) for fun, simply because I wanted to learn more about gemstones, and I was captivated by the hosts' knowledge. In my cubicle at one (non-jewelry-industry) internship, I would browse jewelry websites during my downtime. After college, I pursued a Master of Fine Arts degree in Creative Writing, and my training in writing and storytelling naturally lent itself to marketing. After completing graduate school, I decided to teach college-level writing part-time and followed that career path for half a decade until I realized that I didn't want to pursue a PhD, which I'd need to advance my teaching career. Throughout those years, while trying to make ends meet financially, I was always taking on freelance marketing projects and learning about different industries and brands along the way.

A quarter-life crisis inspired me to leave the New York City metro area for Los Angeles, which attracted me with its sunshine, creative energy, and vibrant jewelry industry. During that transition period, I quit my primary teaching job and took a part-time role as a retail sales associate at a jewelry store. There, I was able to focus on learning about jewelry sales. In addition, my employer gave me the opportunity to become Diamond Certified through the Diamond Council of America, and I completed some coursework through the Gemological Institute of America or GIA. After moving to Los Angeles, I decided to pair my diverse experience in marketing with my overflowing passion for jewelry and began offering my services to jewelry brands exclusively.

I named my business Joy Joya for a few different reasons. First, I really wanted to communicate my belief that marketing can be approachable and even fun. I want the clients I serve to know that marketing can also help them pursue their joy and passion, since it can enable them to grow their jewelry businesses. In addition, the word "joya" means "jewel" in Spanish, a language I love deeply; in college, I earned a minor degree in Spanish language and literature. I like how "joya" contains the word "joy", even though you can't hear it, since the "j" is pronounced like "h". The two words together allow me to express my vision and values to you.

Now that I've had the chance to truly immerse myself in the industry, I've come to realize why I was so drawn to it in the first place and why I love working with jewelry brands; so many of them are founded by creative and visionary entrepreneurs who have a unique perspective on fashion and design. In addition, many of these entrepreneurs - especially up-and-coming independent designers - are women, and I love surrounding myself with fierce and sparkling feminine energy.

For many years, I struggled to make sense of how I could monetize my creativity, more specifically my talent and skills in creative writing, so I get what it's like to be stuck in "starving artist" mode. I know from my experience and observation that many jewelry business owners – especially the independent designers selling directly to the consumer – also struggle to balance creativity with strategy.

While I still consider myself to be a highly creative person, I'm sure that my higher calling is to help other creative people realize their visions and fulfill their dreams. At some point in my career, I took the Gallup CliftonStrengths assessment, and it confirmed an inkling that I had about myself: my top professional strengths are "Strategic" and "Relator". It's true I have a knack for strategy and for seeing the big picture. However, I also find immense joy in developing and maintaining strong, meaningful relationships, not only between me and my clients but also between brands and their customers.

FINDING JOY IN MARKETING

CHAPTER ONE

WHAT IS MARKETING?

Marketing refers to the effort any given business makes to create and maintain relationships with its target and current customers. Businesses build relationships with their customers by communicating their stories, offering value, reinforcing their brand presence, and demonstrating consistency and reliability. Marketing can occur across a number of platforms and through various approaches, some of which can be digital. Within digital marketing, there are many different subtypes of marketing, including search marketing, content marketing, social media marketing, email marketing, influencer marketing, event marketing, and more. I'll define all these subtypes later in this book.

Why is marketing important for jewelry brands?

Marketing is important for every brand, even the most established and well-known global brands. Consumer needs and demands change rapidly, especially in our digital-first world. As a result, brands must learn how to pivot quickly and adjust their marketing messages to meet consumers where they are. Otherwise, they risk losing market share to a quick and nimble newcomer who isn't afraid to push the marketing boundaries - and knows the value of doing so.

Getting noticed as a jewelry business is harder than ever before. If you don't have a clear brand, value proposition, and marketing strategy, then you're definitely going to get lost in the noise. Experimenting with different marketing tactics and hoping they work is not going to help you compete with new brands entering the marketplace with investment backing and a solid marketing strategy and team.

Despite the saturation in the marketplace, opportunities do exist, if you understand how marketing can help you take advantage of them. Digital marketing puts the power of creativity in everyone's hands, so up-and-coming brands can not only be creative in their marketing efforts but also extremely unique and disruptive. If you can set realistic goals and then follow through on your plans to achieve those goals, the sky's the limit for your jewelry brand.

B2B vs. B2C vs. D2C

I understand that some jewelry entrepreneurs reading this book may be selling their products to retailers, while others may be selling directly to the consumer. I would like to clarify the differences between the terms "B2B" and "B2C" and then explain how marketing will vary for each business model.

B2B stands for "business to business", referring to a jewelry wholesaler. A B2B jewelry brand is either manufacturing the jewelry products and selling to retailers for resale, or they're serving as the middleman between the manufacturer and the retailer. In addition, a B2B brand in the jewelry industry may be a service provider, like a company that sells appraisal software for jewelers. B2C, on the other hand, stands for "business to consumer" and is a general term that refers to any jewelry brand selling products to end consumers. More specifically, D2C is any jewelry brand selling its products directly to consumers without a middle-man wholesaler.

The marketing strategies that work well for B2C jewelry brands don't always work for B2B jewelry brands and vice versa. To complicate matters further, some jewelry brands are considered both B2C and B2B, so they must segment their marketing efforts accordingly to appeal to more than one target audience. B2B and B2C brands build different types of relationships with their customers. In general (but not always), B2C jewelry brands are focused more on serving their customers, while B2B brands are focused more on supporting their customers.

If you're a B2C jewelry brand, you'll want to constantly be asking yourself the question, "How am I serving the customer and his or her needs?" Often times you'll feel tempted to push your own agenda on your customers because you think you know what they want. However, marketing for B2C is about all about listening. Pay attention to customer feedback, develop products the customer actually wants to buy, and offer real value. Then use your marketing message to communicate your attentiveness.

In B2B marketing, the marketing initiatives that work best are content-driven. If you can provide valuable, informative, and compelling content as a B2B brand, then you will naturally attract the right customers to you, since they'll be looking for a supportive partner to help them grow their business.

B2C customers rarely buy jewelry solely for its technical features, especially since most consumers typically don't know enough about jewelry materials and manufacturing techniques to be that discerning about them. When B2C customers decide to make a purchase, they're doing so because they've gotten caught up in a powerful feeling, or they're buying into a certain lifestyle.

For example, your average consumer does not purchase a diamond engagement ring solely because of the diamond's carat weight, clarity, cut, and color. Of course, those factors may play a role in helping a consumer choose between one diamond and another. Instead, a person buys a diamond engagement ring because of what it represents and how it will make the recipient feel: loved, cherished, special, and worthy of such a thoughtful and expensive and meaningful gift.

On the other hand, B2B customers buy jewelry not because they're moved by it but because they see potential in making a profit from it. Of course, many B2B jewelry buyers purchase jewelry because they like it. But they also want to know about the quality and origin of the materials, the manufacturing process, and more. As a result, B2B jewelry brands must use their marketing efforts to educate their customers rather than to evoke emotion.

As I mentioned above, many B2C customers aren't as informed about jewelry industry jargon as B2B buyers. While some B2C customers, perhaps those shopping for bridal jewelry, may know the difference between a claw prong and round prong, most will have no idea how to distinguish one from the other. They'll simply know that they like how a piece of jewelry looks when it's presented to them.

You'll want to speak in a language the customer understands, using words that evoke feelings. If you look at an engagement ring product description from

a D2C brand like Tiffany & Co., you'll find something poetic like this on their ecommerce site: "Just
as the sun's rays radiate outward, casting light in
every direction, so too does the Tiffany Soleste® engagement ring. With a scintillating halo of brilliant
diamonds and a striking emerald-cut center stone
featuring concentric rows of parallel facets, light is
gathered and mirrored throughout the design, resulting in an unrivaled display of brilliance."[3] Of course,
you'll want to include specs for your jewelry pieces,
but you can leave those for the product details.

On the other hand, a B2B buyer likely doesn't
have time for figurative language and branded "fluff".
That person will want to cut to the chase and understand how your jewelry is different from your
competitor's jewelry in terms of durability, quality,
and value. Specs, product options, style numbers,
turnaround times, and prices matter. If you look at
engagement ring semi-mounting product pages for
B2B jewelry brands like Stuller, Overnight Mount-
ings, and Quality Gold, you won't see any product
descriptions at all. You'll simply see product render-
ings, a style number, and all the technical specs.

As you can see, the best practices for B2B and
B2C marketing differ, but the goals for both are the
same: to capture attention, to motivate the customer
to buy, and to create long-lasting relationships. Giv-
en the customers' opposing goals and motivations,
the approaches for reaching customers will vary.

How is marketing different from public relations and sales?

Whereas marketing is about helping a brand create relationships directly with end consumers, public relations – sometimes called press, PR, or publicity – is about creating the strategic relationships that will help a brand manage its image and reputation. For jewelry brands, public relations usually means networking with the press, celebrities, fashion stylists, and influencers, since these people typically decide what's "cool" and relevant at any given time.

A public relations specialist or publicist has a keen ability to connect her brands with editors and influencers. She's always looking for opportunities to place her clients' pieces in the right publications and with the right stylists for celebrity borrowing. She also has her finger on the pulse of trends, so she can pitch her brands and their products accordingly.

Not only do public relations specialists write and submit press releases, but they also send pitches to journalists and seek opportunities for newsworthy stories. In addition, they maintain and manage a jewelry brand's press kits and lookbooks and provide guidance on communications, especially during a crisis. Finally, they manage relationships with stylists and celebrities, they occasionally handle influencer marketing, and they can plan and execute media days or other events related to brand reputation.

While marketing is the process of creating aware-ness and getting a consumer interested in a jewelry brand and its products, sales is the process of turning that newly aware and interested consumer into a paying customer. Marketing attracts and courts cus-tomers, and sales makes the big "ask", going directly for the conversion.

In a brick-and-mortar retail setting, the salesper-son helps guide the shopper, who may have a vague idea of what he or she wants to buy, into making the best purchase. The salesperson educates the shop-per on benefits, features, and pricing. The salesperson keeps the shopper engaged and in the store with the goal of making a sale.

In a B2B setting, the salesperson or team that rep-resents a jewelry brand may travel to retail partners to show the product in person. The salesperson or team may act as a brand representative at a trade show or other industry event. In addition, the B2B sales process may be managed by a third-party that owns and manages a wholesale showroom, which is a space – either physical or digital – that offers a link between a jewelry designer and a global market. Buyers that represent retailers view the products in a showroom and then make the purchasing decisions for the stores they represent.

Without marketing to "warm up" the consumer or retailer, each one of these sales interactions would be cold. However, in an ideal situation, marketing creates awareness so that the salesperson or team can interact with an aware and informed audience, thus increasing the chances of making a sale.

For direct-to-consumer ecommerce brands, sales plays a less traditional role in the buyer's journey because the consumer only interacts with the website, not with a salesperson. As a result, calls to action strategically placed throughout the site and sales-driven email campaigns become important because they invite the consumer to make a purchase after marketing has done its job.

Ideally, you'd be focused on developing all three functions in your jewelry business, so they can work together harmoniously, supporting each other and your growth. If you can only focus on one at a time, you'll need to examine your short-term and long-term goals and then decide which of the three could most effectively help you reach your target customers. Marketing without sales is sometimes too passive, but sales without marketing can feel like shouting into a vast canyon. Public relations without marketing can make a brand seem distant and unattainable, while marketing without PR can sometimes feel self-congratulatory.

Where are you in your marketing journey?

I speak to many jewelry entrepreneurs on a regular basis, and I'm constantly assessing various jewelry brands, from the perspectives of both a consumer and a marketing professional. I know that every brand - even the major players - can stand to improve their marketing in some way. There's always room for growth and improvement! Whether you're trying to raise brand awareness for a fledging jewelry brand, or you're evolving an established legacy brand to meet new consumer demands, you should assess the current state of your marketing and be honest with yourself about your strengths and weaknesses. What are some questions you can ask yourself?

Is your current marketing strategy supporting your business goals?

Are you currently measuring the results of your marketing efforts?

Do you have all the resources you need to execute your marketing plan?

Do you have access to the people who can support you in your marketing efforts?

Do you understand how you should be distributing your marketing budget and prioritizing your marketing efforts?

Do you feel like you're communicating your brand effectively?

Do you understand your brand's unique value proposition?

Do you currently use a calendar to plan your marketing efforts?

Is everyone on your team aware of your business and marketing goals?

Are you utilizing all your sources of marketing data?

If you answered "no" to any of these questions, then you definitely have opportunities available to you. I'm excited for your potential and for the future of your brand!

CHAPTER TWO

THE MARKETING MINDSET

Before you move forward with a new marketing strategy or revise your jewelry brand's current marketing strategy, you will need to adopt the appropriate attitude and mindset in order to manage your expectations and create the optimal conditions for success. To embrace a marketing mindset that will prepare you for growth, you must learn how to embrace uncertainty, be curious and inquisitive, understand and trust the process, let go of the past to make room for change, and remain positive.

Embrace uncertainty

One of the most exciting things about being a marketer is that I can use data to inform and guide most of my decisions, especially in a digital world where data is freely available and plentiful. I can examine how customers behaved or responded in the past and then make educated guesses about how to get customers to take the desired action in the future.

However, marketing isn't a perfect science. Even though I can make educated guesses, I can't read customers' minds, and I can't predict the future. As a result, every marketing initiative has some degree of uncertainty attached to it.

To further complicate matters, some of marketing involves trying something new that's never been done before. When you're striking a new course, you often don't really know what to expect, even if you're devising a strategy based on logic, best practices, industry data, and more. As a result, you should start getting used to uncertainty - because marketing involves a lot of it.

Be curious and inquisitive

The best marketers are extremely inquisitive about human behavior because it's in our best interest to constantly ask questions about what makes people tick. If something didn't work, approach it in a curious way instead of being upset about it. Ask yourself "What if?" and "What about?" questions so that you can try to better understand why something didn't work instead of lamenting your failure. If you already have a passing interest in psychology, then now's the time to explore and embrace it.

Understand and trust the marketing process

Of course, you can outsource all your marketing to a marketing expert and never have to deal with any of it. But ideally, you should at least understand the basics of marketing, since it's so intertwined with other business functions and processes, like product design and development, customer service, and sales. You're taking a positive first step by reading this book!

Furthermore, if you do outsource your marketing, then you'll want to partner with someone you trust. Marketing is a process that, as I mentioned, can involve a lot of uncertainty. You want to partner with someone who, at the end of the day, has your best interest at heart - because you'll experience both ups and downs. You want to trust that marketing is a process and that you can pivot and make changes when necessary. No failure is ever a failure in marketing, since you'll always gain data that will help you make better decisions moving forward.

Let go of the past

You must learn not to let past marketing results dictate how you feel about your potential for future success. Many of my clients admit that they had worked with other marketing providers in the past and were disappointed by the results. As a result, they've adopted a fear-based mindset, and they're typically not as receptive to new advice and may not be open to trying new marketing tactics without the guarantee of some specific result.

If you can't let go of the past, then you won't have a very promising future. Instead, try adopting a growth mindset: if you believe you can achieve better results in the future, then you'll be able to do just that. You will be more open to receiving feedback from customers and marketing partners, and you'll feel more confident about applying that feedback to improve your future marketing efforts. In addition, you'll be more receptive to trying something new, which could end up being the thing that sets you apart from your competitors.

Trust your customers

Many jewelry brands think they know more about their customers than customers know about themselves. However, today's consumers are empowered, and they have endless amounts of information available at their fingertips. Jewelry is a time-honored industry with deep roots, and many of the long-standing players are so blinded by tradition and by what they know has worked in the past that they're not able to pivot their marketing strategies as consumer needs change. They limit themselves by believing they know best.

For example, some bridal jewelry retailers today are sabotaging themselves by only viewing marketing through one lens. The traditional approach has worked for decades: they've been marketing solely to young men, the ones who shop for engagement rings, right? However, so much has changed over the years. Today's bridal jewelry retailers should be marketing to women, many of whom are shopping for themselves and making decisions about their own rings. They should also be marketing more to minorities and to members of the LGBTQ+ community.

Jared is a great example of a jewelry brand that was able to get out of its own way. In 2018, Signet, parent company of jewelry retailer Jared the Galleria of Jewelry, announced that it would be dropping the well-known tagline it had used in advertising campaigns for more than a decade. "He Went to Jared" was replaced with "Dare to Be Devoted".[4] The new tagline allows Jared to communicate the emotional element of buying and gifting jewelry in a nongendered way. By paying attention to your customers and realizing they know better about what they want and need than you do, you can accommodate them accordingly.

Remain positive

Always judge your results as they relate to your original marketing goals and never out of frustration or other negative emotions. For example, if you didn't get as many Instagram followers as you wanted in one week, you haven't necessarily failed. The lack of new followers could mean absolutely nothing, especially if your final goal is to generate sales (maybe your sales ultimately won't even come from Instagram, and that's okay). Marketing requires patience, so remaining positive will help you feel better about the long haul. To remain positive, stay focused on your long-term goals and how your marketing efforts are helping you achieve those goals.

What marketing can - and can't - do

Unfortunately, too many jewelry business owners have unrealistic expectations about what marketing can achieve, especially on a compressed timeline. They hope that the right marketing initiative will be able to solve long-standing problems. Marketing can't erase years of poor customer service practices, add sparkle to a lackluster product assortment, or put a bandage on a flawed business model. Marketing does have its limitations, and in order to demonstrate favorable results, it needs to harmoniously work hand-in-hand with all other business processes. Once you understand what marketing can and can't do, then you can use marketing more effectively, in a thoughtful and strategic way.

What marketing can do

1. Marketing can introduce you to the marketplace. Are you debuting your jewelry brand? Are you releasing new products or collections? Marketing

can get you in front of the people who should know about you. In this way, you can think of marketing as a debutante ball: your brand is ready for its big debut, and you're dressing it up in a fancy gown and presenting it to society.

2. Marketing can get your jewelry brand in front of new customers. At some point in time, you may realize that you'd like to penetrate new markets. Do you dream of reaching a global audience? Would you like to target a new age demographic? Marketing can help you connect with those new customers.

3. Marketing can get your jewelry brand in front of customers the moment it matters, like when you're running a promotion or releasing a new product or collection. In some instances, you may feel it's even more important than usual to communicate with your customers. For example, if you're having a sale, introducing new products, or hosting an event, then you'll definitely want to send a time-sensitive message to the right people.

4. Marketing can help you build relationships and trust with prospective and existing customers. According to Edelman's "Trust Barometer" report from 2019, trust drives brand loyalty: 82% of survey respondents said they will continue to buy from a brand they trust, even if another brand suddenly becomes more popular.[5] Once you earn a consumer's

trust, you're more likely to keep him or her as a life-long customer. Marketing can help you build and nurture that trust.

5. Marketing can help you portray your jewelry brand in the best way possible. You already think that your jewelry is awesome and that people should buy it. However, sometimes the awesomeness of your jewelry can be difficult to communicate, especially if the consumer is not able to try it on or even view it in person. Marketing can help you portray your jewelry in the best light and support how your designs tie into your brand story.

6. Marketing supports sales efforts. Marketing cannot replace sales initiatives, but it can support your sales team and goals by ensuring that customers are actually seeing the jewelry and becoming familiar with your brand. This way, when your salespeople interact with customers, or your sales messaging includes a direct call to action, less friction will exist, since the consumer will already be primed for the sales pitch.

7. Marketing can support your customer experience by delighting your customers. Marketing can't serve as a substitute for exceptional customer service, but it can support it. If you're interested in providing an overall fantastic customer experience, then you can create some more out-of-the-box marketing campaigns that entertain and intrigue the

customer, making him or her more curious about your brand and products.

8. Marketing can educate and inform your customers. What do you want your customers to know about your materials, your design process, your values, and more? Marketing can teach and inform your customer, and it can answer any questions he or she might have about your brand before even thinking to ask those questions.

What Marketing Can't Do

1. Marketing can't make any customer buy from you. Wouldn't it be nice if marketing could be the little voice in the customer's head that says, "Buy!"? However, that's simply not what marketing does. Not being able to sell any of your jewelry is a frustrating experience, but marketing isn't and will never be a quick fix. Customers have free will.

2. Marketing can't make you an overnight success. A marketing strategy takes time to develop and execute. In addition, with some marketing strategies, you won't begin reaping the results until months or years after you implement the marketing strategy. John Jantsch from the blog Duct Tape Marketing writes "...it is likely going to take six months to a year for you to see the kind of long term momentum that you want. The kind of momentum that has peo-

ple talking about you and commenting that they see you everywhere. Marketing is a living and evolving system. Marketing can't improve broken sales processes".[6] Buckle up: you're going to be in this for the long haul.

3. Marketing can't make an undesirable product seem more appealing. If no one likes your product, then no amount of marketing will make people want to buy it. Of course, marketing is a great way to test whether one target customer is drawn to your product. You can quickly pivot and test a new target customer if the original one proves to be a less-than-ideal fit. However, marketing can't change a lame product.

4. Marketing can't fix unattractive price points. Are you stuck at a specific price point and wondering why people aren't buying? Marketing can potentially get you in front of the people who are willing to spend the money you're asking them to spend, but it won't fix a price point that doesn't appeal to anyone. Instead, you'll have to revisit your product development process and make a new product at a different price point, or you'll need to reconsider your pricing altogether.

5. Marketing can't make up for a lack of business strategy. If you're lacking a solid business strategy, then marketing won't be able to patch the mistakes and missing pieces.

6. Marketing can't immediately fix long-standing reputation issues. Do you have a poor reputation among customers because you've provided less-than-stellar customer service, or your products didn't hold up to the claims you made about them? If so, you've likely collected some negative reviews about your business. Marketing won't erase the bad taste in the customer's mouth.

7. Marketing can't substitute for poor customer service. Similarly, if your customer service team isn't providing an exceptional customer experience, then your marketing won't be able to keep customers happy, satisfied, and wanting to buy more.

8. Marketing can't alleviate your fear of change. If you're not constantly evolving and innovating to keep up with your customers' needs and desires, then marketing can't transform you into a cutting-edge business with its finger on the pulse of its customers. Of course, marketing can provide you with the opportunity to describe your business as innovative or forward-thinking, but most savvy customers will be able to see through your facade once they start interacting with you.

In summary, marketing must work in harmony with all the moving parts of your jewelry business - sales, customer service, product design and development, and more. It can't replace any of these moving parts, and it can't carry the weight of something else that isn't working.

CHAPTER THREE

DATA AND RESEARCH

Before you can build the marketing strategy and plan for your jewelry business, you must do your research in order to understand your place in the market and your target customers. Research should also inform your product development process and help you set realistic goals. Depending on whether you're a new jewelry brand or an established one, you'll have various amounts of data available to you. For example, a jewelry brand that's been in business for five years will be able to draw from a larger pool of data than a brand-new jewelry business. Regardless, a jewelry brand at any stage can use data to help inform marketing decisions.

With each one of your business' digital footprints, you're generating heaps of data, from your ecommerce store and your social media presence to your email marketing, digital advertising campaigns, and beyond. Data can feel overwhelming, but it's powerful in the hands of business owners and leaders who know how to use it.

According to a report from Ascend2 and Research Partners, the top two reasons that marketers use data are: to feel confident about making decisions based on data analysis and to acquire new customers.[7] Do you often feel confused about what to do next in your marketing strategy? Do you wonder, "Where do my target customers spend their time, and how can I reach them effectively?" The answers to these questions lie in your data.

Data protection and privacy in jewelry marketing

If you collect email addresses on your website or sell anything from your ecommerce storefront, then you have access to sensitive data that your customers would definitely not want exposed. Jewelry businesses of every size - even the small ones - should be actively protecting customer data and addressing their customers' privacy concerns. No business is immune to data breaches and cyber-attacks.

Over the past few years, a number of jewelry brands have been impacted by data breaches, which can occur as a result of internal error or external foul play. In December 2018, Signet Jewelers was impacted by a data breach that allowed any person to view the order information of other customers by slightly modifying the link included in the order confirmation email.[8] A year later, ecommerce jewelry brand

Missoma announced to its customers in an email that malicious software from a third party had targeted their payments page and "inserted a code that was designed to capture information entered during the checkout process".[9] In 2020, the accessories retailer Claire's suffered an ecommerce breach when hackers used payment skimmers to steal customer data.[10]

As a jewelry brand, you need to care about data protection just as much as you care about the customer experience because the two support one another. Today's consumers - your target customers - are seriously worried about their data. According to a report from Pew Research Center, 79% of Americans are concerned about how their data is being used by companies.[11] You should care too if you want to build a long-term relationship with your customers based on trust and respect.

Many consumers don't actually understand that your careful storage of their customer data is helping you give them exactly what they want: a more personalized, convenient, and fun shopping experience. 90% of U.S. consumers find marketing personalization very or somewhat appealing, but many don't realize that their data is the price they pay for it.[12] Storing and leveraging the data you have about your customers is one of the best ways to serve them. As you provide your customers with as much value as possible, you also have a major responsibility to use their data carefully while respecting their privacy and maintaining transparency.

Not only should you care about data protection and privacy for your customers' sake, but you should also care about data for the sake of your business reputation and to safeguard yourself from legal troubles. Breaking the laws of data protection and privacy can leave you vulnerable to hefty fines, penalties, and other legal consequences, which could put your business and livelihood at risk.

Transparency

When it comes to marketing in 2020 and beyond, transparency is key for so many reasons. Not only do today's consumers want to know everything about a company's supply chain and about the social causes that company supports, but they also want to know how their data is being handled and used. As a result, you must be open and honest about that information.

Posting a generic privacy policy on your website is simply not good enough. Instead, you should be proactively sharing information about how you're protecting customer data and actively letting your customers know how their information is being used. For example, instead of promising your customers they'll receive occasional notices about promotions in exchange for their email addresses, be specific and let them know how often you send emails, giving them the chance to adjust their email preferences.

Privacy regulations

You'll definitely want to familiarize yourself with privacy regulations, both in the US and globally, so you can achieve compliance and be knowledgeable when customer questions and concerns arise. For example, the PCI DSS, or Payment Card Industry Data Security Standard, is a set of standards created by credit card issuers to ensure secure credit card transactions online. If you sell anything online, you must adhere to the PCI DSS standards. The Federal Trade Commission or FTC also has its own privacy and security guidelines.

The most stringent of the privacy regulations is the European Union's General Data Protection Regulation or GDPR, which went into effect on May 25, 2018. Just because your business is based in the US doesn't mean you're exempt from the regulations; the GDPR encompasses anyone who sells products to customers in the EU or that collects data from those individuals. GDPR requires marketers to follow strict guidelines, especially when it comes to email marketing. The cost of failing to comply can be high. According to the Financial Times, "Regulators in the U.K. have levied $126 million in fines for data violations since instituting new stronger privacy mandates in mid-2018".[13] Again, no business is immune to the risks and consequences.

Opportunities

Adhering to data privacy rules and regulations may seem daunting and overwhelming, but it actually presents great opportunities and can challenge you to strengthen your marketing strategy in accordance with best practices. Consider the fact that having access to your customer data is a privilege and not a right. As long as you can handle and manage customer data responsibly, then you'll be able to maintain access to it. If you break the rules, then you'll lose your privilege - and forfeit an important tool in your marketing arsenal.

Furthermore, data privacy rules and regulations force you to gain true consent from everyone who receives your marketing communications. For example, every subscriber on your email list should be someone who has willfully agreed to receive your emails and who doesn't unsubscribe. This is actually great! As a brand, you only want to be marketing to people who are genuinely qualified to be your customers. Otherwise, what's the point? Why would you want to spam people who don't want to hear from you? Privacy rules and regulations can help you trim your customer list, so you can send more specific and targeted emails to the right people.

Finally, data privacy rules and regulations can encourage a culture of transparency within your business operations. If you follow the guidelines and best practices outlined by the GDPR and other organizations, then you'll immediately begin conducting business in a more transparent and accessible way. Today's consumers, now savvier than ever before, will appreciate your openness and your concern for both their identity and privacy. You'll build a foundation of trust and earn their respect and loyalty over time.

Gathering - and making sense of - data

What role should data play in your jewelry marketing strategy specifically, and how can you start using data in a more intentional and proactive way? Some common data sources for jewelry brands - especially e-commerce brands - include Google Analytics, organic and paid social media data, customer sales and customer experience data, and email marketing data.

Google Analytics

A free service provided by Google, Google Analytics (GA) is one of the most powerful tools that ecommerce jewelry brands can use, since it allows them to monitor and track a multitude of online shopping behaviors. For example, with GA a jewelry brand can see how many prospective customers are visiting the ecommerce store within any given time frame, understand how those prospects are finding the store, view how much time prospects spend on various pages, and see how many customers are abandoning shopping carts instead of finalizing their purchases.

If you're not already tracking website behavior with GA, then you simply have to install a small section of code on the backend of your website – that's it! Not only can you customize your reports based on your individual needs and goals, but you can also set actionable goals before you launch any given marketing campaign.

Organic and paid social media data

Facebook (and Instagram) want to provide you with lots of data about your jewelry business because they ultimately want you to advertise with them. As a result, you can easily find data insights about your social media posts. Thanks to these insights, you can get a sense for which types of content perform better than others and also gauge your audience demographics. If you'd like to access more comprehensive data and reports about your social media accounts, then you can try a paid tool like Iconosquare.

Do you already run Facebook and Instagram advertising campaigns? If so, then you'll definitely want to pay attention to your data. Not only does this data help you determine whether or not you're spending your ad budget efficiently, but it can also provide you with additional insights about your target customers. Furthermore, it can help you understand the media assets and copywriting that best resonate with those customers. With its detailed targeting capabilities, Facebook advertising can also be a great way for your brand to test a new market before you commit to it.

Customer sales and customer experience data

If you run an ecommerce jewelry store, then you're sitting on a goldmine of customer data that brick-and-mortar store owners often can't access unless they're diligent about maintaining their customer records. In order to make a purchase, your ecommerce customers need to submit a certain amount of information about themselves. You also collect data about customers' path-to-purchase via tools like Google Analytics and Shopify (or whatever ecommerce platform you use).

Once you know more about your customers' browsing and purchase history, then you can further personalize and tailor your offerings to satisfy their wants and needs. You can segment your customers by behavior and other characteristics and then precisely target your marketing messages. In addition, you can make adjustments to your product assortment and merchandising strategy based on customer activity.

You should also be tracking data related to customer experience, which refers to how a customer feels when interacting with your brand, making a purchase, or reaching out to your customer service team. To do this, you can monitor your online reviews, send surveys, and analyze your customer retention rate. Remember: it costs more to acquire a new customer than it does to win back an existing one, so you should put a lot of time and effort into monitoring the customer experience and ensuring that it's consistently a positive one.

Email marketing

Your email marketing list is like gold; of course, you always want to be winning over new customers, but you also want to spend as much time winning over new email subscribers, since those subscribers are the prospects you'll be nurturing and converting into your future customers.

If you're not paying attention to the data from your email marketing efforts, then you're missing out on major opportunities to build long-term relationships with prospects and current customers. An email marketing platform like Mailchimp can provide you with invaluable data like open rate, click-through rate, unsubscribe rate, and more, so you can assess the strength of your email marketing efforts and then make adjustments to future campaigns. Furthermore, you can test your email campaigns to discover whether one type of messaging is more effective than another type.

Market research

Market research is another powerful way to gain data, but it deserves its own section, since it's so customizable and scalable. Are you struggling to understand your customers? Are you wondering how to move forward with your product development strategy? Market research can provide you with the data you need to get unstuck, so you can confidently plan a strategy for forging ahead. When conducting market research, you have the option to pursue primary research and secondary research.

Primary research

Primary research refers to research you conduct yourself, like focus groups, online surveys, observation, and product testing.

Focus groups: In a focus group, a small but diverse group of people is assembled for a guided or free discussion about a brand or specific product. Typically, you'd want to assemble a group of people from your target audience, unless you're trying to gain more insights about who your target customer is. Businesses like conducting focus group because they can talk to the customers directly, and the format is typically open-ended and flexible. However, the organizer must have clear goals in mind, prepare prompts and questions, and use an experienced moderator. Today, you can even find platforms to conduct virtual focus groups, which can save you money and help you be more flexible about who you'd like to participate in your focus group.

Online surveys: Online surveys are one of the easiest and most budget-friendly ways to conduct market research. However, you'll need a pool of people to participate. In addition, you'll likely need to offer some incentive in order to inspire your recipients to take the survey. Tools like Survey Monkey and Google Forms make it easy for you to put together a survey for a low cost or even for free. You may want to work with someone who has experience creating effective surveys, since writing the right survey questions is an art - you'll need to tease out the information you want to know in an inviting way. If you don't have an email list of contacts, then you can hire a service like PeopleFish, which will find survey participants for you, as long as you create the survey. Finally, many social media platforms like Instagram and Facebook have survey features, so you can informally ask your followers questions.

Observation: If you really don't have a budget for market research, or you're starting from scratch, then you may simply want to engage in some observation. For example, you can spend some time on Instagram and take notes about your perceived competitors' social media data. Which of their posts seems to be the most popular? What types of comments are followers leaving on their posts? Who are they targeting with their posts? What are people saying about your competitors' products? You can check review sites like Facebook, Yelp, or Google Reviews, or you can look at individual product ratings and reviews.

Product testing: Are you trying to get a sense of the viability of your new product or collection? Would you like to know if it holds up to wear and whether or not your target customer would like it? Would you like to know how your customers style and wear your products? If so, you may want to move forward with product testing. You can test a limited run of your products with customers at a pop-up shop or live event. You can offer the product to your VIP customers at a discounted price. You can lend to friends, family, or employees. If you have an e-commerce store as well as a brick-and-mortar store, you can test your product online on a drop-ship basis before you bring it into your store inventory.

Secondary research

On the other hand, secondary research refers to research that has already been done, like articles, references, and reports. What are some places where jewelry brands can find secondary market research? Industry publications like *JCK* and *INSTORE* are great places to start. You'll also want to look at *WWD*, *National Jeweler*, and *Retail Dive*. Finally, you can simply Google any information you'd like to know. You can find benchmarks and statistics for the ecommerce retail industry and beyond. I always recommend filtering Google search results by the past year, so you can ensure that you're seeing the most recent information. Finally, always consider your source and make sure you're looking at information from credible publications.

Among my jewelry brand clients, I find there's a common misconception about market research: that it's expensive. However, that's simply not true. Hiring a market research firm will cost about $15,000 to $35,000, but you don't have to spend that much, at least not at the beginning; one of the best things about market research is that you can scale it accordingly. If you really lack a budget, then you can focus on consulting secondary sources, which are plentifully available on the Internet. However, if you're feeling creative and have a little bit of money to invest, you can try polling your customers on Instagram or via SurveyMonkey, sending a survey email to your top customers and offering an incentive to complete that survey, being more open to observation, or simply talking to target customers at live events.

Ultimately, where you seek your data and how you decide to track it will depend on your individual business and marketing goals. If you don't have a goal in mind, then you won't be able to designate one or more key performance indicators, and your data will look like nothing more than a meaningless bucket of numbers.

A/B testing

When you graduated from school, you probably thought you were finally done with tests. I hate to break it to you: if you'd like to develop a successful marketing strategy for your jewelry brand, then you're going to have to do a few more tests. A/B testing is basically an experiment that helps you better understand what is and isn't resonating with your target audience. If you've never tried A/B testing, then all your marketing efforts are the result of your best guess. Wouldn't you like to be able to make more informed decisions about where to invest your attention and marketing dollars?

A/B testing is best for testing your ecommerce website, email campaigns, and social media ads. By testing each one of these channels, you can better gauge the effectiveness of elements like copywriting, calls to action, images, video, email subject lines, and more.

A/B testing for ecommerce optimization

We'll discuss ecommerce optimization further in Chapter 17, but here's some background information about testing. If you run an ecommerce store for your jewelry brand, then you likely change and update it based on customer feedback and intuition. What if you could create two different versions of your homepage, important landing page, or even a product page to see which one results in more conversions? You may be surprised to discover that changing the color of a button or adjusting the text in your call to action can inspire more customers to buy products instead of abandoning their carts.

Here's one example: the ecommerce jewelry store The GLD Shop was able to achieve a 300% increase in conversion rate just by adding a new welcome pop-up to their homepage.[14] Building on some existing design elements, the ecommerce optimization agency Justuno created an alternative pop-up that's larger and utilizes different fonts and colors. However, they maintained the same discount offer on both pop-ups and used the percentage discount as the control for the experiment. When they ran the A/B test, they saw that the new pop-up outperformed the old one, and they could feel confident about implementing it.

A/B testing for email campaigns

In Chapter 11, we'll delve further into email marketing, but here's a taste of how you can use A/B testing to boost your email campaigns. Have you been feeling disappointed by the results of your email marketing efforts? You can try A/B testing your emails by experimenting with different subject lines, calls to action, images, send time, and more. In fact, if you already use Mailchimp for your email marketing campaigns, then A/B testing is easy; it's included in the Essentials, Standard, and Premium plans.

A/B testing works best with a list of at least 5,000 subscribers, so you may need to beef up your mailing list before you can fully take advantage of A/B testing. However, even if you haven't reached that level, you should still be familiar with how A/B testing works.

To begin A/B testing in Mailchimp, you simply create your email, specify that you'd like to run a test, choose the variables you'd like to test (subject line, from name, content, or send time), decide how you'd like to split the recipients, and choose how to determine a winning email. For example, winners can be based on open rate, click rate, or other metrics.

A/B testing for social media ads

You'll learn more about social media advertising in Chapter 9, but here's some info about testing ads. For many brands, one of the easiest ways to engage is A/B testing is to apply it to a social media advertising strategy. When running a Facebook ad campaign for their jewelry brand, many jewelry business owners aren't sure which imagery to choose or which captions to write.

The next time you run a campaign, try A/B testing! Once you decide on your campaign objective and select your target demographic, you can start by creating an ad with one image. Then, create one or two duplicate ads with the same image and write different captions for each one.

Throughout the duration of your advertising campaign, you will not only know which images are the most effective, but you'll also be able to gauge the better image/caption combo. After the campaign has ended, you can apply your insights to the next campaign.

Getting started with A/B testing

So how can you start with A/B testing? Let's go back to school. You may remember from science class that one of the first steps in setting up an experiment is to form the hypothesis. If you can't seem to remember how to do that, then you'll definitely want to check out Craig Sullivan's Hypothesis Kit.[15] His simple kit includes three segments that you can modify based on your needs. They include:

1. Because we saw (data/feedback)

2. We expect that (change) will cause (impact)

3. We'll measure this using (data metric)

Here's one example of how it can all work together for a jewelry brand: Because we saw that Image #1 with Caption #3 copy performed the best, we expect that creating a new campaign with similar images and slight variations on the copy will result in more effective ads. We'll measure this data using Facebook Business Manager.

Recommended tools

Google Optimize: Did you know that Google Optimize will allow you to test variants of your web pages and see how they perform per your hypothesis? One of the best things about Optimize is that it works closely with Google Analytics. In addition, one version of Optimize is actually free!

Optimizely: If you would like to invest more money into your A/B testing, then you can consider using a tool like Optimizely, which is considered the world's leading experimentation platform. Even someone who doesn't have technical skills can create their first test quickly and easily.

Shopify apps: Do you run your ecommerce store on the Shopify platform? If so, you can try some of the Shopify apps for A/B testing, which include Neat A/B Testing and Products A/B Test. While the former allows you to test your pricing, copy, images, product page layouts, and homepage layout, the latter allows you to split test your product details and pricing.

With A/B testing, you lack reasons to keep guessing about your marketing efforts. Once you know the results of your tests, you can better reach your customers and watch your sales grow.

Competitive analysis

Now that you know how to conduct research and where to access data, you'll want to either define or redefine your competitors before you finalize your marketing strategy and move forward with a marketing plan. Since the market is constantly evolving, with new players entering all the time, you'll want to revisit your competitive analysis regularly. Furthermore, different marketing strategies may require different competitive research, since not all competitors are competing with you at all times and in all the same ways.

Do you know your competitors? You may have a vague idea of who they are, but if you haven't clearly identified them and studied them, then you haven't done your due diligence. Your competitors aren't necessarily the brands making products that look like yours (in fact, they better not be, since you have a unique product to offer!). Instead, they're the brands already selling products to the customers you want to convert.

To conduct competitive analysis and ultimately get a better sense of the marketplace, you'll want to perform the following steps:

List all your potential competitors: As I mentioned, you probably have an idea of who your competitors are. Make a list. Then, start doing some Google searches because you'll likely find at least one brand you didn't even know existed. For example, if you sell delicate gold and colored gemstone jewelry, then you can Google "delicate gold and gemstone bracelets" and comb through the results. More than likely, you'll find a brand or two that's new to you. Once you identify these unknown brands, you should visit their websites and assess their current marketing efforts. If the brand isn't maintaining the standard that you'd like to maintain, then you shouldn't consider that brand to be a competitor. For each potential competitor, write a short overview about why you consider that brand to be a competitor; a paragraph is sufficient. That way, you can better understand your logic and reasoning. Remember that each competitor might be a competitor for different reasons.

Do a deep dive: For each one of your competitors (you may want to focus on 3-5 to be more specific), you'll want to do a deep dive. Examine the following: their target customers, their pricing strategy, their sales channels (including any retailers), their current branding and digital marketing strategy, the shopping experience, and their strengths and weaknesses.

Target customers: One way you can better understand your competitors' target customers is to view the competitors' social media profiles and any paid advertising they're currently doing. Visit the Instagram and Facebook profiles and perform a casual analysis. Who are the followers? Do they seem to be women with children, or do they skew younger? What types of models are they using in their imagery? What is the messaging? Do they segment the messaging for different platforms and sales channels? In addition, if they're a larger brand, you may be able to find secondary sources, including interviews with executives and even case studies about the brand.

Pricing strategy: Uncovering your competitors' pricing strategies is as easy as visiting their website and looking at their various categories and how they're pricing those categories. What's the minimum price point, and what are some of the more expensive pieces? Make note of these things.

Sales channels: Do your competitors sell online? Are they taking advantage of social commerce? Do they also have a brick-and-mortar presence? Do they only sell direct-to-consumer, or are they also stocked by other retailers? These are all questions you can answer in order to get a better sense of your competitors' sales channels.

Branding and digital marketing strategy: You'll want to make observations about the current brand image and marketing efforts. Is the brand consistent across all customer touchpoints? Can you clearly understand what you competitor is trying to communicate? Do you understand the unique value proposition? Furthermore, you'll want to analyze all the current ways that your competitor is marketing, from social media and email marketing to paid advertising, events, influencer marketing, content marketing, and more. What are the follower counts? Do the followers seem engaged and responsive? Do you see any missed opportunities? What seems confusing or incongruent to you?

Online shopping experience: If your competitor has an e-commerce store, then you'll want to try "shopping" the site, even if you don't buy anything. Do you like the experience? Is it easy to find and learn more about products, or is the site difficult to navigate? How's the checkout experience? How are the product photos and descriptions? Do you see clear policies? Is it easy to contact a customer service specialist?

Strengths and weaknesses: This is your opportunity to review all the above observations and then decide what your competitor is already doing well and what your competitor could be doing better. If your competitor is already doing something really well, then it may not even be worth trying to compete. However, if you notice weaknesses, then you could be discovering opportunities for your brand to differentiate itself and succeed.

Customer personas

Now that you know your competitors, you'll also want to get to know your customers. More often than not, when I consult with a new client for the first time, the client will say, "I don't need to create customer personas because I already know my customers like the back of my hand. Why should I have to commit that information to paper?".

You probably do have a good idea of who your customers are, but you won't be able to scale your business if you can't easily share your customer profiles with your team members and outside collaborators - like photographers, graphic designers, retailers, and other consultants. In addition, you'll struggle when you're ready to set up paid advertising campaigns in Facebook Business Manager or Google Ads, since you won't know how to segment your target demographics for testing.

If you can open yourself to the idea of creating formalized customer personas, then you may even be surprised by how little you know about your customers. You may also find many missed opportunities in your marketing. If you'd like to reach new markets, then customer personas can help you understand the customers you're hoping to reach, so you can adjust your messaging accordingly.

JEWELRY MARKETING JOY · 51

When you're ready to create your customer personas, you can refer back to the beginning of this chapter, since you'll want to consult many data sources in order to define your target customers and understand them more intimately. To get important information about your target customers, you can survey them, review any Google Analytics data you may have, leverage Facebook Audience Insights, look at your Instagram demographics, and more.

Survey your customers

As we mentioned earlier in this chapter, you can use surveys to begin to determine your target customer and what she wants. Ask the relevant questions in a short survey and then send it to your email subscribers. If you want to ensure that people are taking the time to answer your survey, then offer an incentive. If you want to make your survey more fun and casual, consider using Instagram Stories to poll your followers. Polling is an excellent way to engage your target customers and involve them in your business decisions.

Review Google Analytics data

Again, Google Analytics is a powerful source for insights about your target customers. With Google Analytics, you can learn many things about the people visiting your jewelry brand's website, including their geographical location, their age, their gender, the language they speak, the devices they're using to view your site, the pages they visit, how they found your website, and more. To start accessing demographic information in your GA account, click Audience - Demographics - Overview. You may need to enable Demographics if it's not already enabled within your account. You'll be able to see the ages of people visiting your site and the gender breakdown.

Leverage social media insights

In an effort to push its advertising opportunities, Facebook created a tool called Audience Insights. This tool allows you to view information like demographics, pages likes, location, and more for three different groups of people: people on Facebook (the general Facebook audience), people connected to your Page or event, and people in Custom Audiences you've already created. Though it may take some time for you to get enough data to see information about people connected to your Page, you can still take advantage of some of the more general insights in the meantime. Within Instagram, you can also view Audience Insights.

Observe your competitors

Now that you've taken the time to study your competitors, you have more information about their customers. Your ultimate goal is to steal market share from your competitors, so it's in your best interest to know their customers too. It's basically impossible to access confidential sales and market research data from your competitors, so you'll simply have to use what's available – and their social media platforms are a great place to start. On Instagram, for example, scroll through your competitor's follower list and make observations about the users you see there. You may also want to look at the comments on Instagram posts to see the types of things that people are saying about your competitor's photos.

Use your intuition and experience

Your intuition and experience may not be as exact as science, but you should have a general sense of who your customers are, especially if you're a jewelry brand that's been in business for six months or more. As the owner of the jewelry business, you've likely interacted with customers and have had the chance to get to know them better. While you shouldn't rely solely on intuition and experience for market research, you can use them as supplements and allow them to guide you when the data seems incongruous or doesn't make sense.

Now decide what you'd like to know about your customers – and what information will help you reach them. Typically, a jewelry brand should want to know things like age, income, shopping habits and motivations, style preferences, brand affinities, and general interests. Once you have the right information, you can use that information to guide decisions you make about your marketing, including which social media platforms to use, what types of models to include in photoshoots, and what tone to use in the copy, among other things.

When I create customer personas for clients, I build a true three-dimensional view of who these people might be. My report includes the following elements:

Name: I like to actually give the customer persona a name because it serves as a reminder that the persona represents a real human being.

Demographic background: This includes typical demographic information, like location, age, marital status, education, income, etc. However, I like to be as descriptive as possible and write this section as if it's a story about the customer rather than a simple bulleted list of facts.

A day in the life: From the moment they wake up to the moment they go to bed, how do your customers occupy their time? This can be a paragraph to a full page. You want to truly get a sense for how your customer moves through a typical day.

Social media and online behavior: Which social media platforms do your customers use? Where do they spend their time online, including the websites they browse and how often they check email and various social media sites? Do they like to share actively, or are they more passive users? Do they belong to any specific online communities?

Influences: Who influences your customers? Are they influenced by friends and family members, or are they influenced by social media influencers? Who do they ask for recommendations? What resources do they consult before making any purchase, especially a major purchase? How long does it take them to make a decision, and how many steps does the decision usually involve?

Shopping frustrations: What do they hate about shopping, and what are their pain points? How could shopping be easier for them? Do they prefer to shop online or in store? What level of customer service do they require?

Brand affinities: What are their favorite brands and even their brand loyalties?

As your product assortment grows and changes, you may want to reconsider your target customer and perform market research on a semi-regular basis, since what was true six months ago may no longer be true. That being said, taking the time to try to understand your customers is much more important than ignoring them and simply hoping that someone will buy your jewelry.

PRODUCT AND PRICING

*"Don't find customers for your products,
find products for your customers."*
Seth Godin

Product development

Marketing begins long before any marketing campaigns actually get executed, way before the social media posts, email campaigns, blogging, events, or advertising. It even begins before you create a marketing strategy and plan. The truth is that effective marketing actually begins with product development.

If you want to have a successful jewelry business, then you need to realize that your marketing must be built on a foundation of strategic product development with a viable pricing strategy, so you can ensure that you're making the products that will inspire your customers to open their wallets for you - again and again.

Before you decide that you want to invest in your business and commit to selling your new, existing, or updated jewelry products to your target customers, you will want to ask yourself some important questions.

Wait...jewelry's a product?

Many people avoid referring to jewelry, especially fine jewelry, as a "product" because it's made with such care and artistry. It's not a roll of toilet paper, so isn't it more art than product? Anything that you plan to sell in the marketplace is a product and should be considered as such.

Why would someone buy our jewelry instead of another brand's jewelry?

The answer to this question can't be, "because we made it". As the creator of your jewelry, you definitely think it's special. Of course, your jewelry is your baby, the best thing since sliced bread. But do you target customers see it that way? Your jewelry must be unique and attractive beyond the fact that it's new and created by you.

Does our jewelry have an interesting story behind it?

More than likely, your jewelry does have an interesting story. However, some brands need to work harder than other brands to uncover that story. If you can't pinpoint and communicate your story, then you'll struggle to create a marketing strategy and distinguish your brand in the marketplace. You may need to work with a professional to help you tease out what's most interesting about your brand, and you'll want to extract the details that will most appeal to your target customers.

Is our jewelry memorable and recognizable?

The marketplace is saturated with jewelry brands that think they're unique and memorable, but the truth is that, if you were to dump all this jewelry in a huge pile, you would probably have a hard time distinguishing one brand from another because so much jewelry looks the same. Strive to be the jewelry brand that's easy to recognize in a crowd.

Does our jewelry appeal to a niche market?

By "niche market", I don't mean all women between the ages of 20-60. I mean, markets like "urban women in their 30s who love abstract contemporary art and desire sculptural accessories". You can get even more specific and target a community like "marathon runners who wear motivational jewelry when they run". It may seem cheesy and uncool to target niche audiences because you're trying to build an empire, right? And empires appeal to everyone, right? Not today, they don't. You can build an extremely profitable business by targeting a specific niche.

Are we pushing boundaries, or can we be more innovative?

If you're simply riding the coattails of another popular jewelry brand, and you think you can surf that wave of popularity all the way to the bank, then you're in for a rude awakening. For example, if you were making bangle bracelets a la ALEX AND ANI in 2012 but selling them for less money, you may have been able to thrive for a short period of time. But you probably wouldn't still be in business today. ALEX AND ANI isn't as popular as it used to be, but most people still recognize the brand. Your knockoff brand, on the other hand, is a distant memory. Create something unique that you can continue building and evolving for many years to come. Create something that other knockoff brands will want to emulate. Push yourself to be more innovative so that everyone else will want to copy you.

When you're having trouble sparking innovation within yourself or your product development team, or you feel stuck about how you can create products that will resonate with your target customers, then you may want to look outside the jewelry industry for inspiration. Many companies today begin with a vague idea of how they want to reach their customers. However, after some time, most realize that they will need to adapt and pivot in order to match the true needs of the marketplace. By studying examples of many successful companies in other industries, you may feel inspired to breathe more innovation into your own jewelry business. For example, did you know Starbucks started in 1971 by selling espresso makers and coffee machines? These days, they sell lattes on nearly every street corner, it seems. That shift didn't happen overnight. Instead, it required a lot of testing and experiments, listening to customer feedback, and the commitment to constant evolution.

If you don't really know the answers to the questions I just asked, or you don't think you can answer them confidently, you may need to go back to the drawing board before launching your jewelry business. I would highly recommend you read the book *Purple Cow* by Seth Godin, which is one of my favorite books about marketing – and it's not even really about marketing at all. It's about creating remarkable products so that marketing those products can come naturally. Here's one great quote from the book: "The old rule was this: create safe, ordinary products and combine them with great marketing. The new rule is: create remarkable products that the right people seek out."[16]

If you want to be relevant this year and beyond, then you need to impress your target customers with products that inspire awe and delight. Once you create those products, then you can test them with your target market. You can sell the pieces in a soft launch or lend them to friends, family members, and even employees, so they can wear them for a short period of time and then provide you with feedback about wearability. In addition, your subjects can also let you know if the pieces attracted attention or compliments. If the test pieces aren't performing the way you thought they would, you may want to redesign them or rethink your target customer.

Pricing strategy

Unfortunately, just because your customers like the look of your products doesn't mean they'll be willing to spend the money you're charging for those products. Once you have viable products that you know your customers will want to buy, you'll need to devise an appropriate pricing strategy. The right prices won't undervalue your brand, but they'll also feel reasonable for your target customer, whether that customer is an aspirational buyer who can't yet afford luxury or the self-purchaser who treats herself to a big-ticket item once per year.

Before you can decide on how to price your products, you need to make sure you have a solid business plan, that you've identified and studied your competitors, and that you've specifically described your target customers. When devising your jewelry pricing strategy, you'll want to consider quantifiable factors like your cost of labor, cost of materials, and any overhead associated with making and selling the product, like tax, freight, ecommerce website fees, etc. In addition, you'll want to be clear on how you'll be selling your jewelry. Will you be selling only through your ecommerce website, through retail partners, or through multiple channels? All these factors will play a role in how you price your products.

What are your competitors' price points? In order to differentiate yourself from them, you may want to offer slightly lower price points by developing products that will still enable you to make a profit without compromising too much on quality or attractiveness. Alternatively, you may want to match your competitors' price points and differentiate yourself with your unique value proposition, your brand story, and your customer experience.

What can your customers afford, and when are you pushing their upper limits? Once you know your customers intimately, you'll know exactly what they feel comfortable spending on an impulse buy and what they feel comfortable spending when they're treating themselves. You'll want to develop products that can be priced at those points.

Deciding very early whether you're going to sell exclusively direct to consumer or partner with retailers plays an extremely important role in your pricing strategy. You can decide to sell direct to consumer in order to undercut the competitors who have more overhead than you, but you'll need to realize that you won't be able to suddenly transition to wholesale, since your lower price points aren't factoring in the retail markup. Furthermore, you need to be realistic about the fact that selling direct to consumer won't necessarily mean you'll get to pocket all the cash that would typically go to your retail partners. Instead, you'll have to work even harder to market your brand, so you'll need to reinvest a large portion of your margin in marketing.

For additional insights about pricing, I spoke to Nan Lung Palmer, a jewelry industry consultant who specializes in merchandising and pricing. She said that the number you get from your pricing formula isn't necessarily the number that will resonate with your target customers. For example, if you're using extremely high-quality materials, then your material costs will be high and drive up the cost of the product. A bracelet that should cost $200 if you want to appeal to an aspirational jewelry-buying customer may suddenly become $800 because you decided to use the best-quality diamonds instead of cubic zirconia. As a result, you will end up alienating your aspirational customer, who can't afford it. You'll need to use some common sense and decide, "Will my customer actually want to buy this piece at the price point I need to charge?" If you can't confidently say "yes", then you'll either want to scrap the design completely, replace the materials, or rethink your supply chain.

In addition, Nan explained that the number you get from your pricing formula may not support an exceptional customer experience. Let's say you offer one gold ring with a dozen different gemstone variations. Given the variable cost of gemstones, your pricing formula will yield a different price for each variation. However, before you decide on your final pricing, you should consider how frustrating it must be for your customer to browse the various options on your product page and see so many different price points! In this type of situation, you need to have some wiggle room. Instead of overwhelming your customer, you may simply want to offer one price point for all the gemstone colors. You may end up with some "loss leaders", as Nan calls them, but you'll make up for the losses by selling other variants. Alternatively, you could also offer tiered pricing: six gemstone variants could have one price, and six could have another price.

Pricing your "hero" products, or the products you know will be your best sellers, will also require you to have some wiggle room. You can price this hero product lower than your typical pricing formula would suggest, since you know this product will sell like hotcakes, and you'll make up for any margin loss in sales volume. Basically, the moral of the story is that you should never be pricing your products using an inflexible formula.

Furthermore, Nan told me that jewelry brands should be getting samples from multiple factories before making their final manufacturing decisions. Currently, it may cost you $3 to make a piece, but what if you could reduce your cost to $2.75 per piece? Depending on the quantity you order, you could be saving thousands of dollars. Nan also asserts that you should seek factories specializing in your niche. Some factories outsource their work, so you could be dealing with a middleman - and overpaying - without even knowing it.

Pricing strategy is an intricate dance, and it balances many different factors at once. To make matters more complicated, you must also consider how any changes to your products or pricing may compromise or alter your brand reputation, which you've worked so hard to build. For example, offering discounts too readily can create the expectation that customers should wait for the next discount and never pay full price. As a general rule, fine jewelry brands should not be offering discounts for first-time purchases, since the discount can come across as "cheap" and devalue the brand. Instead, they should focus on customer retention and offer VIP discounts or some other kind of loyalty program. Fashion jewelry brands don't stand to lose as much by offering discounts to first-time shoppers, since the buyer's journey is shorter, and they can acquire new customers at a more rapid pace than a fine jewelry brand.

At the end of the day, you need to be making at least a margin of 50-60%, or you just have an expensive hobby, as Nan likes to remind everyone. In the fine jewelry industry, some insiders turn up their noses at fashion brands that are creating low-priced products with lower-quality materials. However, these days, fashion brands are making some of the biggest profits, since they can turn over a massive amount of inventory priced at $100 or less. Fine jewelry brands could stand to learn a thing or two about supply chain efficiency and customer acquisition from fashion brands.

One final thing to remember about pricing is that consumers want transparency about pricing. If you're thinking about hiding your prices for whatever reason, ask yourself, "What purpose does this serve?" Today's consumers want transparency about practically everything related to your business, from where you're sourcing your materials to what social movements you support. Here's a great example from the fashion industry: when they launched in 2010, clothing brand Everlane kind of shocked everyone with their "radical transparency" approach. On the "About" page of their website, they write, "We believe our customers have a right to know how much their clothes cost to make. We reveal the true costs behind all of our products—from materials to labor to transportation—then offer them to you, minus the traditional retail markup."[17] Then they break down the cost of some of their best-selling products, taking into consideration factors like materials, labor, and transport and then showing how their retail markup compares to traditional retail markup. Today's jewelry brands could stand to be more radical about their price transparency and look to companies like Everlane for inspiration.

CHOOSING YOUR MARKETING ADVENTURE

CHAPTER FIVE

BRANDING

Some people have trouble wrapping their heads around the concept of a "brand", since it's an intangible thing. A brand is a feeling we get when we interact with a business and/or its products and services. A brand is not only an identity, but it's also an essence. A brand ensures that all your customers perceive your business, products, and services in a unified way, so that those things can be recognized even in a sea of competitors. You can think of brand as a "vibe", "energy", or *je ne sais quoi*.

According to data from Lucidpress, "Brands with consistent branding expect to earn 23% more annual revenue than the brands that are inconsistent."[18] Consistency means extending your brand to all your consumer touch points, from your website and social media profiles to all your print and digital marketing collateral. It also means being consistent every single time – with every social post, every email, every blog post, every new product addition, every paid advertisement, and more. Your consistency is what your customers will come to expect from you.

Difference between "brand" and "branding"

To clarify, since I'll be using both terms here, there's a difference between "brand" and "branding". While the former is a noun, the latter is the verb. A brand is basically your business' personality; however, the action of achieving and continually refining that personality is branding. Yes, it's a continuous effort, and yes, it can and should evolve over time. If you're new to the marketplace, then you'll need to devise a brand from scratch. You'll have the opportunity to get it right the first time, and you'll be able to create a brand that will resonate with your target customers and distinguish you from your competitors. However, if you're an established jewelry business, and you're not sure that your brand is truly representing your identity, then you may need to make some important changes. Updating your brand can be tricky, since you'll be disrupting how your customers are used to seeing you. Rebranding is the process of reinventing an outdated brand.

Brands evolve over time

After an "unsatisfactory" 2018, jewelry brand Pandora decided that it was time to reinvent itself. Executives admitted that the brand had high brand awareness but lacked brand identity, based on a survey of 28,000 customers.[19] Pandora illustrates the differences between brand awareness and brand identity and why it matters.

In the case of Pandora, many of their customers - and even people who have never bought from the brand - are highly aware of the "Pandora" name. For the most part, they know that Pandora is a jewelry brand, and they've probably seen a brick-and-mortar store location in their local mall or have seen an ad for Pandora in a magazine. They may also know that Pandora, at least at one point in time, was well known for its charm jewelry and that charms are highly giftable. Pandora's brand awareness is still excellent, even today.

These days, I don't see as many people wearing Pandora's signature charm bracelets, even though it was a widespread trend at its height in about 2016. The look has fallen out of style, and women are no longer scrambling to fill their bracelets with new charms.

Today, many people continue to see and recognize the Pandora brand, but they may wonder, "What do they even sell anymore? Are they still relevant?" At the height of the brand's popularity and the charm bracelet trend, Pandora had both brand awareness and brand identity. Consumers recognized the brand's name, and they knew they could visit a Pandora store to buy a starter charm bracelet or add-on charms, for themselves or for a loved one. The word "Pandora" was synonymous with charms.

Over time, even the most loyal consumers were no longer charmed by charms – and not necessarily interested in trying something new. The brand awareness remained, but the brand identity became unclear. Currently, Pandora is working hard to redefine target markets and create new products that will reach new customers; they also had to consider their brand positioning. They're trying to redefine who they are and then communicate their new identity to current and prospective customers.

As a jewelry brand, why should you care about this story? Most importantly, it serves as a cautionary tale for the importance of monitoring both your brand awareness and brand identity, at every stage of growth – and then acting accordingly to maintain balance.

If you're a new jewelry brand, then you probably have the opposite problem that Pandora has. You're working to build your brand identity, but you have very little brand awareness. At this point, you may want to focus less on solidifying your identity and place more attention on getting your brand noticed. Over time, you can return to your brand identity and make adjustments based on the feedback you get from new customers.

Your brand identity can help you generate awareness, especially when it's memorable and noticeable. However, you can take steps to get your brand identity in front of more people, so you don't have to just cross your fingers and hope that customers will find you. You can reinforce brand identity and build brand awareness through tactics like advertising, social media marketing, email marketing, event marketing, customer interaction, public relations, and more. You also don't want to forget that your employees are a part of your brand identity and that they have the power to spread brand awareness. When you hire new employees, you'll want to make sure that they support your culture and mission, since they'll be some of your best brand ambassadors, especially if they enjoy working for you.

If you're curious about your current level of brand awareness, you can take steps to measure it. Like Pandora, you can survey customers. Or, you can conduct a focus group, monitor your web traffic, and pay attention to social media mentions/comments and product reviews.

Finally, you'll also want to keep brand positioning in mind. While brand identity is the feeling customers have when interacting you, and brand awareness is your reach, then brand positioning is the way your brand maintains "fast feet" in the marketplace. You must always be looking at trends, customer desires, competitors' offerings, changing customer life circumstances, shopping habits, technology, customer expectations, and more. For example, today you may have a favorable brand identity among millennials, and you're able to reach them effectively through Instagram, creating a high level of brand awareness. However, if you're playing the long game, you'll want to anticipate that your customers will eventually get older - maybe they'll have families and less time to spend on Instagram. Maybe they'll simply have different priorities than shopping, or they'll want different types of products. Will you change your product offerings to reach that same segment of customers, or will you try to reach another generation of customers? Your brand must be nimble and adaptable. It's a living and breathing entity that needs constant attention.

Once you feel like you've achieved a balance between brand awareness and brand identity, you'll want to realize that managing your brand isn't a one-and-done process. In fact, your brand identity can change overnight, in both positive and negative ways. You need to be actively monitoring customer perceptions and then making small or major adjustments, depending on how well your brand identity is aligning with your target audience. You'll want to continue checking in on your equilibrium and asking yourself important questions, including:

Am I growing too quickly and losing my brand identity in favor of brand awareness?

Am I introducing too many new products too quickly?

Am I trying to evolve in ways that confuse the customer?

Do my customers even want the new things I'm planning to offer them?

Having strong brand awareness and brand identity allows you to build customer-based brand equity. A term first coined by Kevin Lane Keller in 1993, "customer-based brand equity"[20] refers to the value of your brand through your customers' eyes. By building your customer-based brand equity, you will create a loyal customer base that feels comfortable trusting and recommending your jewelry brand. The more equity you can build, the more growth you'll experience. If you're feeling overwhelmed by building brand equity, then you can start on a local level within your community and expand your reach from there; it's a more manageable way to approach the brand-equity-building process. Once you build equity, then you can also ask more from your customers; you can potentially sell products at higher price points and cultivate prestige and exclusivity, two qualities that are especially important for luxury brands.

Design matters in branding, especially for a design-driven business

As you can imagine, when it comes to crafting an impactful brand identity for your jewelry brand, design is everything, since brand identity is the ultimate visual representation of your brand. Does your brand identity capture and convey everything you want your customers to know about your mission, values, and products?

In one scene of the Oscar-award-winning film *Parasite*, a rich businessman is intrigued when his chauffeur hands him a business card for VIP concierge services. Knowing nothing about the company, the rich businessman looks at the sleek logo and decides immediately, based on the design, that the concierge company must be very reputable and exclusive, even though that's actually not true (I don't want to spoil too much!).

Most, if not all, jewelry business owners already know about the importance of design when it comes to their product assortment, but not all of them are extending that mindset to their brand. According to Adobe's State of Create 2016 report, 59% of consumers will choose to do business with a company over one of its competitors based on good design, and 45% of consumers have even paid more for a product or service with good design.[21] In an industry as saturated as jewelry, you're doing yourself a disservice by not paying attention to design, since so many jewelry brands – both big and small – are already making it a top priority. Good design is usable, so it's easy to understand and navigate without too much thought. Good design follows design principles like contrast, balance, proportion, emphasis, hierarchy, repetition, rhythm, pattern, white space, movement, variety, and unity.

Taking risks with your brand

If you've been feeling a sense of *deja vu* lately, you're not the only one. More luxury brands are taking fewer creative risks with their logos, websites, and Instagram feeds. Have you seen Burberry's latest logo? It has joined brands like Diane von Furstenberg, Balenciaga, and Saint Laurent, which are all sporting the all-caps, sans-serif "wordmarks" or "logotypes", meaning their logos are built entirely of the word or words that make up the company name.[22] While the original logos for these brands were unique (albeit dated), the fonts for the new logos all look very similar and even nearly identical for someone who may not be familiar with the nuances of fonts.

This same-same approach may work for brands that are already basically household names, but what should an up-and-coming jewelry brand do? No-frills logotype logos look very elegant and refined when they're stamped on jewelry boxes, but let's face it – they're not very memorable. If your jewelry brand has this type of logo, customers who aren't familiar with your jewelry brand will likely assume that you're some sort of luxury brand – but will they know what sets you apart from your competition?

To make matters worse, many jewelry brand websites are starting to look the same, since most are built on Shopify and follow similar standards and design practices. On one hand, copycat websites are less problematic than copycat logos because websites should be built around user experience and best practices – and best practices are best practices for good reasons. What works for the top e-commerce websites will likely work well for all websites. At the same time, if your website looks like every other jewelry website, you may be doing yourself a disservice, since you won't be able to distinguish yourself in any memorable way. A look like clean minimalism may be a trend, but a brand aesthetic must support the story and core values of any given brand. Don't be a copycat just because the strategy seems to be working for other brands.

"Blanding"[23] or bland branding (a term coined in 2018 by Thierry Brunfaut and Tom Greenwood) is worrisome but not necessarily surprising. Brands are playing it safe, choosing the approach "if it's not broken, don't fix it." But if you truly want to make a splash in the marketplace, especially one as saturated as jewelry, you need to stand out visually.

What are the most common brand elements?

In actuality, many moving parts support a brand, and they've been strategically arranged to elicit an effortless feeling. These moving parts include your business name, logo, color palette, photography, product designs, packaging, pricing, history, customer service, customer experience, communications, and more.

Logo

Of course, a brand is more than its logo, but a logo plays an important role in brand identity. An effective logo should distinguish your jewelry brand from your competition, inspire curiosity, be unique and memorable, and be related to your brand. Logos usually only have one to two colors, but they should also work in black and white, in case your marketing collateral requires that. You can use text only in your logo or incorporate a symbol. Also, you should be aware that your logo may change and evolve over time, and that's okay. Even some of the world's most recognizable brands in the world, like Google, have updated their logos over time.

Color Palette

Take a moment to imagine the color that represents Tiffany & Co.'s brand identity. If you were able to see Tiffany Blue like a robin's egg, then you know first-hand how a color can represent a brand. When choosing a color palette for your brand, you'll want to select one-to-three dominant colors and then three-to-five accent colors. The number of colors you choose will depend on the amount of color variations you'd like in your brand identity. You won't necessarily use all the colors on every page of your website, in every version of your logo, and on every piece of marketing collateral, but a predetermined color palette will give you options. In general, you'll want to know that some of the most common brand colors include blue, green, and red. While blue represents trustworthiness and loyalty, green symbolizes growth and freshness, and red symbolizes power and passion.

Photo Treatment

As a jewelry brand, so much of your visual identity revolves around photography. You have photos of your products, and you also have photos with models. To make matters more complicated, jewelry photography is a notoriously difficult process, since things like smudges and reflections can distort the quality, while light can change the entire look of a jewelry piece. The overall style of your photos will definitely impact your brand image. Are the photos energetic, or are they minimalist? Are they colorful or more muted? How do you style the photos? What types of models do you use? All these individual de-

JEWELRY MARKETING JOY · 83

tails will eventually add up to create a whole. Your photos should ultimately tell a story. In Chapter 6, we'll discuss photography in greater detail.

Look/tone/feel

To begin building your brand, you'll want to work with a marketing professional or team to create a look/tone/feel, which you'll eventually share with a graphic designer, who will be able to translate your look/tone/feel into a visual identity. Most marketing professionals and graphic designers have their own slight variations on this process, but I like to include the following elements in the look/tone/feel.

Brand mission and values

In your brand mission, you should strive to capture the emotion you'd most like to evoke in your customers. For example, your business' mission might be to "create affordable fine jewelry for everyday wear", but your brand mission should strike a deeper chord, like "empower women by giving them the opportunity to express themselves in a playful way."

Your brand values should capture the reasons why someone might buy from you as opposed to a competitor who sells a similar product. For example, your customers may choose you because you value trust and transparency, and you're always clear about how you source your materials.

Look

The "look" portion of your look/tone/feel document will cover elements like design style, fonts, colors, model guidelines, and product photography guidelines. If you don't feel like you have the language to describe these elements, you can start by making bullet points or compiling screenshots of other brands that capture what you'd like to achieve. Then, during a later stage in the brand development process, a marketing consultant or graphic designer can help you flesh out your initial thoughts.

Don't be afraid to describe your design style using adjectives you might use to describe a person: quietly alluring, feminine, luxurious, outgoing, etc. After all, your brand is a personality, and you should feel like you're creating a character who will play the central role in an epic story.

One great place to start looking for font inspiration is Type Wolf or typespiration. If you're not sure about the colors you'd like to associate with your brand, try Adobe Color, which allows you to view color palettes based on the color wheel. You can also upload an image you like to Adobe Color, and the tool will extract the image's dominant colors.

Become an observer of other brands. Make a list of all the brands you admire, no matter what the reason. Then, comb through their branding and marketing efforts: visit their websites, shop their product pages, pick up a print catalog if applicable, and subscribe to their emails. Make mental notes about how these brands use color, font, models, and photography. Then, you can borrow details that resonate with you and ignore the ones you don't like.

Tone

Your brand's "tone" refers to how you speak to your customers on your website, in your product descriptions, in your email marketing, in your social media posts, in any other forms of content marketing, and in paid advertisements.

You'll want to set the communication goals and standards for your brand voice. When you communicate with your customers, what do you want them to take away from the exchange? Would you like them to understand your brand mission, feel ignited by your enthusiasm, or develop a sense of trust? Then, which adjectives would you use to describe your voice, and which words feel appropriate, i.e. casual slang or more formal, multisyllabic words?

If you're struggling to understand tone, think of your favorite people and the way they speak. Do they gesture with their hands, or are they more subdued, preferring to share only a few well-chosen words? The way they speak and communicate is likely in line with their personality.

Feel

The "feel" part of the look/tone/feel document refers to the overall feeling you want customers to have when they interact with your brand. Do you want your customers to feel inspired, happy, refreshed, relaxed, encouraged, trusting, confident, or acknowledged? Whatever it is, you should articulate it and always strive to make customers feel that way.

Once you have a look/tone/feel in place, you'll be better prepared to communicate with your graphic designer, who will create assets like your logo and any other visual elements. Your graphic designer will also translate your look/tone/feel and translate it into a brand style guide or brand identity guide, which will help you remain consistent in all your branding and ensure that you always follow the "rules" of your brand.

Your customers will know you first and foremost by your brand identity, so you'll want to do everything in your power to build a memorable and positive brand that can also grow with you as you scale your jewelry business. A look/tone/feel document plays an essential role in that process.

Typically, a graphic designer can help you create a brand identity from start to finish, and you can use the look/tone/feel as an outline to help communicate your goals and vision to the designer. This process of working with a designer begins with a brand audit. During this audit, the designer reviews the current state of your brand (if it already exists) and then analyzes the things it's already doing well, along with what could be improved. In addition, the designer can make recommendations about how the brand should optimally position itself in the marketplace. Next, the designer will usually host a brand kickoff workshop (terminology may vary), during which you and the designer will engage in a deep-dive discussion to better understand the foundation of the business as well its goals, expectations, and hopes. After this, the designer will typically present a mood board, to ensure that he or she has interpreted the look/tone/feel effectively and that everyone is on the same page. From there, the designer will create a logotype and brand system, which includes the logo, typography, color palette, secondary graphics, iconography, photography style, and illustration style, if applicable. After that, the designer will present you with your brand style guide, which is the final "rule book" for your brand. It ensures that your look/tone/feel remains consistent and explains how your brand should present itself to the world through its logo, font and color selections, photography, and more. Before designing any new creative assets, launching new marketing campaigns, or working with a photographer, you should always consult the brand style guide.

CHAPTER SIX

COMMUNICATING YOUR BRAND

Once you've established your brand identity, you'll need to decide exactly how you're going to communicate it with your target customers, so they can get to know your jewelry brand. You'll be able to share your identity through the written word, photos, videos, and other visual graphics. In this chapter, I'll be sharing all the best practices for telling the story of your brand, so you can maintain consistency across all customer touchpoints while building trust and recognition.

Using language effectively

When you're communicating your brand identity, the majority of your messaging will be driven by a visual component, since jewelry appeals so much to our sense of sight. However, copywriting still matters, even when pictures or videos are involved. Captions, calls to action, website copy, email copy, and more can all provide context and support the visual story you're trying to tell. Without copywriting, your images and videos live in a vacuum.

To develop a captivating and consistent voice for your brand, you'll definitely need to know your customer first, so you can understand how to speak to him or her. Does your customer resonate with elegant descriptive language, or does this person want the writing to be more conversational? Does your customer want to feel a personal connection with your brand, or does this person prefer a distant, institutional feel? The answers to these questions can help you understand how to speak to your customer in an appealing way. Documenting your brand voice in a style guide will help you remain consistent, and it will also make it easier for you to collaborate with your team members and any outside consultants or partners.

When you begin writing about your brand, you'll have to temporarily forget about your products and get clear on your "why". In his book *Start with Why*, Simon Sinek explains that the most successful and memorable brands put their purpose before their products. Especially today, with consumers from younger generations being more purposeful about their purchases and conscious about how they spend their money, brands need to stand for something. Very rarely a jewelry product on its own is enough to make someone want to buy. Your customers are also choosing to buy your ethos and everything you represent and not necessarily just your product features and specifications.

Next, you'll want to think about telling a story, so you can enchant and seduce your customers instead of selling aggressively. By "story", I don't mean you need to write long strings of paragraphs like you're drafting the next Great American Novel. Instead, you can cultivate some choice phrases and short sentences that express relevant emotions and capture your brand's true essence.

One of the most common mistakes I see is a dependence on too many adjectives. When jewelry brands don't really know how to define themselves, they lean on descriptive terms, and the results are very wordy. Adjectives can sound descriptive and seem like they have substance, but sometimes an adjective really isn't saying anything at all. Instead, try choosing stronger, more specific, and more active nouns. For this exercise, a thesaurus will come in handy. Finally, you'll want to do everything you can to appeal to all the senses and avoid cliches at all costs.

Put yourself in your prospective customer's shoes. He or she knows very little about you and your brand. You'll want all your copywriting to help you establish trust, come across as professional and legitimate, and exude a welcoming tone. How can you guide the customer into making a purchase? Create a sense of urgency and action by inviting the customer to look and learn, especially on your homepage.

If you struggle with writing, then study brands you admire (they don't necessarily have to be jewelry brands) and try to notice what they're doing well with their copywriting and their voice. Practice emulating their approach and put your own spin on it. I also suggest hiring a professional copywriter with experience in the jewelry industry, since this person will have the knowledge and experience necessary to translate your vision into an appropriate and captivating story.

Brand story

Everything starts with a story. Stories give us the power to make sense of our lives and understand our place in both society and history. If we couldn't share our stories, then who would we be? When you're making a new friend or developing a new romantic relationship, you want to dive right in to the other person's story. What makes that person unique? What are some of her passions? How does her past inform her present? What are her dreams?

Similarly, a story is also the heart and soul of your jewelry brand. Not only does a story help you communicate why your brand matters, but it can also help you distinguish your brand from your competitors and give your customers a reason to feel emotionally drawn to you while bonding them to you for the long haul. So how can you craft a story that resonates with your target customers and that represents your true essence?

Traditionally, a story is a narrative with a clear beginning, middle, and end. For many of us, the word "story" equates to the written word. For a jewelry brand, the story could be the text you put on your website's "About" page or the information you include in a press kit or other marketing materials. However, your brand story can also be communicated in so many ways - video, audio, imagery, product, customer service interaction, and more. It can also be communicated through multimedia, which would involve a mix of all those things. However, when you're trying to pin down your story for the first time, you should get back to the basics and begin with a pen and paper (or a blank Google Doc).

Write it all down

First and foremost, you'll want to write as much as you can. Brainstorm wildly. Don't censor yourself and start from the beginning. On a piece of paper, share anything and everything related to the history, values, and mission of your jewelry brand. What influences you? What inspired you to begin? How has your brand changed over time? During this phase, you're not allowed to feel self-conscious about your writing, and you're not allowed to make any edits. Just get it all out.

Look for the feeling

One of the most common mistakes I see when evaluating how jewelry brands are communicating their story is that the stories resemble essays or cover letters for job applications. Throughout our school years, we were trained by our teachers to write reports and essays, so we're used to crafting a thesis and then supporting it with facts and concrete examples.

Too many designers are telling us where they went to school, how many years they spent working for other jewelry brands before deciding to do their own thing, and then listing their technical skills, awards, and experience. Last time I checked, you want your customers to buy jewelry from you, not hire you for a job. The average consumer really doesn't care about these things.

Instead, feel your way through the story. Writing your brand story is an intuitive exercise, and you'll want to try your best to lead with your heart and less with your mind. Reread the lengthy brainstorm you wrote in the first step and try to pick out the parts that resonate with your emotions. If something makes you feel a wave of nostalgia or a twinge or emotion when you reread it, then that detail is probably an important element of your brand story. If you feel too close to your own writing, then ask a trusted friend or family member to read it and invite that person to pick out the parts that are ripe with feeling.

Delete the parts that are too cerebral or resume-like and write a draft that maintains all the touchy-feely parts.

Choose the right details

By the time you're putting together your brand story, you should already have your brand identity in place. You know how your brand looks visually, and you know what you want your customers to feel when they interact with your brand. You know how you need to differentiate yourself from your competitors, and you know exactly who you'd like to attract to your jewelry. Now it's time to gather all your brainstorming and decide how much of it aligns with your brand. How can you shape it into a story that communicates the bigger picture?

Remember that your story won't only just live as a block of text. It will be expressed in all your content, from your products to your lifestyle photos to your social media content and videos. It will come through in what other people say about you and in the legacy you will start to build over time. Make something memorable that you'll feel proud to share with the world.

Slogans and brand taglines

If you were to poll your current customers and ask them to describe your brand in a few words, what would they say? Would each person describe your brand in a different way? When you create a memorable, catchy, and accurate tagline to encapsulate the essence of your brand, you make it easier on yourself to stay consistent with your message and ensure that every customer is having the same experience.

Consider some of the most popular jewelry taglines of all time: "Every kiss begins with Kay" from Kay Jewelers, "A diamond is forever" from DeBeers Group, and the now outdated "He went to Jared" from Jared. Some more contemporary examples from smaller brands include "Quietly bold" from Dana Bronfman and "#ThisIsTheLast jewelry line you'll ever need" from The Last Line. Writing a remarkable tagline means knowing - without a doubt - what your brand represents in the marketplace and getting clear on who will be buying your products.

Challenge yourself to be creative and interesting. Boring or unoriginal taglines result from a lack of confidence or clarity about your brand's unique value proposition. Some brands are afraid to define themselves too specifically because they don't want to alienate potential shoppers. However, being too general won't help you attract the right customers either. Commit to making a clear statement about what the customer can expect when shopping with you, so you can actually deliver on that promise in a genuine way. Ideally, the promise is something only your brand can deliver. Overused, generic taglines like "dainty fine jewelry" and "everyday luxury" just won't cut it in an oversaturated marketplace.

Calls to action

A call to action or CTA is the element in your copywriting that invites the user to take a specific action like "learn more", "shop now", "sign up for email updates", etc. CTAs are typically found on ecommerce homepages, in email marketing campaigns, in advertisements, and in social media posts. To craft an effective CTA, you'll want to start your statement with a strong command verb; shop, learn, sign up, buy, download, subscribe, and order are all very common. Let the user know exactly what you'd like him or her to do in a specific way and then quickly explain the benefit of taking action. You may also want to include a time frame when possible to create a sense of urgency. For example, an effective CTA might read something like this: "Shop now to take advantage of this limited-time sale".

I'll share more specific information about effective copywriting for various platforms - like your ecommerce website, social media profiles, email marketing, and more - in upcoming chapters.

Leveraging jewelry photography

Now that more customers are buying jewelry online, they don't typically have the chance to experience the products in person before making a purchase. If you haven't invested in high-quality photos of your jewelry, then you're probably turning off prospective customers or contributing to your return rate, since your photos aren't accurately representing your products. Not only do you need clear and accurate primary product images, but you also need images that depict the jewelry from multiple angles and on a model. Furthermore, the photos should have a high enough resolution that the customer can enlarge them to view detail. Above all, excellent image quality can not only support your brand identity but can also inspire trust in your target customers, according to one scholarly article written by experts from eBay's Research Labs.[24]

There are actually two types of commercial jewelry photography: product/ecommerce photography and fashion/lifestyle photography. Product photography refers to the types of photos you would find in a printed catalog, on a line sheet, and on a jewelry brand's ecommerce website as the primary photos for each product. On the other hand, fashion/lifestyle photography involves a more creative depiction of the jewelry products. Fashion/lifestyle photography is similar to the type of photography you would see in a magazine editorial, except it's commissioned by a jewelry brand with the goal of selling products. These creative photos can feature colored and textured backgrounds, and they sometimes include models or props. While the goal of product/ecommerce photography is to show detail and scale, the goal of fashion/lifestyle photography is to connect the jewelry products with the brand, to elicit emotion, and to sell a complete lifestyle.

One of the biggest mistakes I see jewelry brands make with their product/ecommerce photography is that they try to get creative with it. Unfortunately, marketplaces like Etsy have normalized this approach to product photography. On Etsy, when a customer searches for any particular type of jewelry, he or she will be bombarded with many different results from a variety of different sellers. In an effort to stand out in those crowded search results, the sellers often try to get creative with their product backgrounds: textured wood, necklace display forms, flowers, colored seamless paper, skin, and more. However, this approach to product photography ends up looking inconsistent, distracting, and unprofessional on a standalone ecommerce website. You'll end up overwhelming your target customer.

To understand and experience the best practices in product photography, you simply have to visit the websites of some of the top jewelry brands. You'll see that Tiffany & Co., for example, doesn't try to get fancy with its product photography. All the products are shot on a plain white background with natural-looking shadows. The products are well-lit, and the details are clear.

Fashion/lifestyle photography is best suited for alternative product images, homepage hero images (the main banner image) and lifestyle photos, social media, advertisements, and email marketing. With fashion/lifestyle photography, you should strive to convey a mood that will appeal to your target customers and attract them to the lifestyle you're trying to sell.

Jewelry is notoriously difficult to photograph, so you definitely want to leave the product photography and digital editing to the professionals. In May 2019, I had the pleasure of interviewing talented jewelry photographer Alain Simic on episode #29 of the Joy Joya Jewelry Marketing Podcast. Not only did Alain shoot the cover photo for this book, but he's also worked with many high-profile jewelry brands, including Midas, DRU. Jewelry, Larkspur + Hawk, and Kendra Pariseault Jewelry. What follows are some edited highlights from the interview, so you can benefit from Alain's wisdom.

Why is jewelry photography so challenging?

Alain: Product photography, still-life photography, and a jewelry shoot on a model are three completely different animals, and in all of those cases it's incredibly important that the jewelry stands out. One thing that's very different about jewelry photography is that you have to work within much tighter constraints. For instance, if you're a fashion photographer, it's sort of limitless what you can do with light and color. With jewelry, you have to be much more careful, obviously, because you're dealing with gemstones and reflective metallic surfaces.

There's a lot of technical stuff that you have to take into consideration. You can't lose sight of the product, which is very easy to do with jewelry because you're working with a much smaller scale.

Why does jewelry photography matter?

Alain: The world that we live in today is completely saturated with imagery, and so much of our lives and our shopping habits are formed by photography because that is the main way we engage with commerce. Much of our lives is digital, so we don't always engage with the product firsthand. It's tremendously important to have high-quality images that can be as much about the product as they are about your brand.

Why must you take ownership of your brand?

Alain: Most jewelry brands, at least from my experience, are not accustomed to having to do so much photography work for their brands. Once upon a time, you would end up in magazine editorials that somebody else shot for you for a publication. Now, to get yourself out there, you have to do a lot more work in producing your own content and varying types of content. You need high-quality imagery, great campaigns, great product photography, and a beautiful looking website. Ultimately all of those elements are going to establish a sense of trust with an audience.

How can you choose a good jewelry photographer?

Alain: Look for a diverse portfolio. If you're looking for a jewelry photographer, and you go to their website and see only one kind of photograph, that's a red flag. I would look for a photographer who has a diverse product photo portfolio. I would want to see many types of jewelry in his or her portfolio. I would want a photographer who has done creative work both within the realm of jewelry and beyond.

I would hesitate to hire somebody who doesn't also produce great creative content that goes beyond the realm of commercial work because in photography it's very easy to get tunnel vision and produce the same stuff over and over again. I would look for a photographer who also produces work that is maybe even abstract or not commercial at all.

No matter how well prepared you are for any kind of shoot, you are inevitably going to run into some sort of technical issue throughout the day. You really want to work with somebody who is experienced enough in this field to be able to overcome those issues.

Why should commercial jewelry photography push boundaries?

Alain: Ultimately, I think the goal for any jewelry designer should be to produce imagery that they themselves haven't seen before or that pushes a little bit away from what they think of as conventional commercial jewelry photography. The goal should always be to cut through the noise, and you don't do that by just repeating what you've seen before. A lot of jewelry conventions that I see in commercial photography, even for larger brands, are a bit dull, and I never see a reason that we can't do something very different. We really have the freedom to do absolutely anything we want. So why would we want to mimic somebody else? I try to push my clients to do something outside of the box.

CHAPTER SEVEN

CONTENT MARKETING

With content marketing, a brand creates and distributes valuable and compelling content that consistently communicates the brand identity and is relevant for the target audience. The ultimate goal of content marketing is to spark and build a relationship with the customer, so that he or she will eventually make a purchase. Content marketing is less about making a sales pitch and more about offering value.

As a consumer of digital media, you definitely come across heaps of content on a daily basis: videos, articles, blog posts, social media posts, webinars, downloadable books, podcasts, quizzes, games, etc. Some of that content is created by brands, while other content is created by media companies. Over time, if you begin to gravitate to a specific type of content produced by a brand, you may start to develop an affinity for that brand, even if you've never purchased products or services from them. You'll begin to trust that brand and feel more inclined to pay attention to what they're selling. You'll soon feel like you're part of their inner circle and consider buying something from them.

That brand didn't have to actively sell anything to you. They simply had to appeal to your senses, whether they entertained, delighted, informed, or inspired you. They communicated a strong message, and you responded accordingly. Instead of seeing that brand as just another business trying to sell you something to you, you acknowledged the brand's efforts to form a genuine relationship with you.

One of my favorite things about content marketing is that it scales easily, so you can start with a very small budget. Statistics from Demand Metric show that content marketing typically costs 62% less than traditional marketing.[25] As long as you have basic skill in content creation and some basic technical know-how - writing, making videos, taking photos, drawing, speaking, etc. - you can get started today. You don't need a content marketing team to begin generating content that works. You simply need some creativity, a solid understanding of your target audience, some time and patience.

Content marketing can take a little longer to work than some other marketing strategies, but it can also be one of the most effective. Marketing expert Neil Patel writes, "You're surely playing a long game by investing in content creation. Traffic, revenue, and audience grow exponentially when it comes to your content strategy- not linearly. At the beginning, you'll grow slowly and will need to add value drops to your content creation pot. Once your pot is filled considerably, you'll start seeing the enormous benefits of content marketing."[26] You won't want to abandon your content marketing strategy after a month just because you're not immediately seeing results.

The other amazing thing about content marketing is that it can build on itself. The more quality content you have, the more website traffic you'll gain over time. Customers will find your content and then discover that you also have tons of other content. They'll start sharing that content with their friends and spend more time with your brand, if only to consume the content you're creating and sharing, and then coming back to spend money with you.

Now that you know about all the benefits of content marketing, you may be wondering how to get started and how to stay consistent with your efforts. At this point, you should already have established a solid brand; you'll want to be completely sure of your voice and the overall feeling you want to communicate to your customers. You should infuse your essence into every bit of content you create, in order to maintain consistency.

In addition, you'll also want to create regular content that's not only consistent but also interesting, unique, and search-engine friendly (we'll get to the search engine stuff in the next chapter). To help you get started, you'll want to consider all content types.

Most people associate "content" with anything related to the written word. Of course, blog posts, white papers, interviews, case studies, and ebooks all fall under the category of content, and they're very typical examples of content marketing today. However, those types of content aren't necessarily so exciting for a consumer-facing jewelry brand to produce and share. Furthermore, content marketing isn't only limited to writing. In fact, content can include video, audio, images, illustrations, GIFs, data visuals, and more. Some of my favorite types of content for jewelry brands include blogs, user-generated content, written and video style guides, behind-the-scenes video, virtual trunk shows and other live video events, interviews, magazines, and more. Continue reading for more information about three of these content types.

Blog

The best part about a blog is that, by its nature, people expect it to be updated regularly. If someone enjoys your blog content, then he or she will return for more. Unfortunately, the word "blog" just doesn't seem as cool as it did in 2009. However, I think the primary reason that blogs are so disappointing is because most brands aren't focused on creating true value with their content. Blogging doesn't only just have to involve words. It can be interactive and include photos, audio, and video. In addition, blog posts can cover a wide variety of topics that either directly or indirectly relate to the brand. They're easy to share, they can serve as gateways to other content and product pages, and they can also be used as bait to get customers' email addresses. In addition, blog posts can serve to improve your search engine ranking if you're optimizing them correctly with the right keywords.

Virtual events

No one could have predicted how the COVID-19 outbreak of 2020 would completely decimate the events industry and everyone who depended on events to get in front of their target customers. Luckily, we already have the technology in place to host events virtually, and consumers are always looking for new digital content and ways to engage with brands and communities. You don't even necessarily have to make your virtual event a sales-driven event. I've seen business leaders and owners use their business' Instagram Live account to interact with customers in completely unique and unexpected ways unrelated to jewelry; the brand's founder may share her workout with her personal trainer or cook one of her favorite meals. If you're able to record video and host it on a platform like YouTube, then that content can be repurposed in many ways. You can share clips on social media, make sound bites, use quotes, pull still images, etc.

I'll provide some more details about event marketing in Chapter 12.

User-generated or user-directed content

Your customers are also an excellent source of content inspiration. Not only can your customers create content for you, in the form of video testimonials, written testimonials, photos of themselves wearing jewelry, and more, but they can also give you ideas. For example, if you frequently receive the same question from your customers, you may want to consider adding an FAQ page to your website or even writing a blog post that provides an in-depth answer to that question. Being in tune with your customers' needs will enable you to produce content that provides value and that will rank highly in search engine results, since your prospective customers are already searching for it.

Content brainstorming and planning

Make a list of all the types of content you consume and would like your customers to consume and then brainstorm relevant ideas for each one. For example, next to the content category of "video", you can include ideas like "brand story video", "video launching our new collection", and "behind-the-scenes video".

Once you've brainstormed a list of content ideas, you'll want to think about how you can share your content strategically. You'll also want to think about where your target customers spend the most time. Some content is meant to stand on its own in an evergreen way, while other content assets may work as a piece of a larger puzzle, so they build on other pieces of content. Some content revolves around certain seasons, promotions, product launches, events, milestones, holidays, etc. Your content marketing strategy will also change, grow, and evolve as your brand grows and as you learn more about your audience.

To give yourself some structure and to help you start making sense of your content brainstorm, you'll want to create a content marketing calendar. You likely already have a calendar for your business or your production schedule, so you can easily incorporate your content marketing calendar into whatever system you already use, whether that's a Google Calendar or some other type of calendar. On this content marketing calendar, you'll want to list all the relevant dates for your business, like milestones, product and collection launches, trade show/trunk show dates, and any other pertinent events. Then, you'll also want to add important retail holidays like Christmas, Valentine's Day, and Mother's Day. And remember to list birthstones for every month.

Finally, you'll want to consider adding social media holidays, which are "holidays" that mostly exist on social media platforms and are promoted through hashtags. To see a very comprehensive list of these holidays, visit the National Day Calendar website. Some social media holidays that may apply to jewelry brands include National Piercing Day (May 16th), National Pink Day (for pink gemstones and/or rose gold, June 23rd), and National #OOTD Day (perfect to showcase how jewelry fits into an "outfit of the day", June 30th).

You'll want to decide where you'd like to place content on the calendar and how it will support whatever goals you have for that period of time. If the content requires any planning or lead time, then you'll want to budget for those things on your calendar, so you're ready to release it when the time comes. Planning ahead in this way definitely requires some forethought, but it will help you stay consistent, since you'll always know what's coming next and feel prepared for it.

Keep in mind that your content marketing calendar should also overlap with your social media marketing calendar and email marketing calendar, which I'll discuss in Chapters 9 and 11. You never want your content to live in a vacuum. In an ideal world, you'll be able to repurpose your content and cross-promote it, to get as much mileage out of it as possible. All your content must work together in harmony.

As you start creating and sharing content, you'll begin to notice that some content will resonate more with your audience than other content. You can use your data in Google Analytics to see what performs the best. Then, you'll want to keep creating more of that type of content and adjusting your plan accordingly.

CHAPTER EIGHT

SEARCH MARKETING

Search marketing is an umbrella term that refers to the process of leveraging search engines like Google to get your target customers to your website. Search marketing encompasses two methodologies: search engine optimization (SEO) and pay per click (PPC).

Google Analytics, Google Search Console, and Page Speed Insights

Offered for free by Google, Google Analytics is a web analytics platform that allows you to view data related to your website and/or app traffic. Not only does Google Analytics help you better understand your customers, but it also gives you insights into your most popular pages and products, customer behavior, abandoned cart rate, and more. You can see how people are finding your site and make educated guesses about why they're leaving instead of buying. The reason Google offers this powerful platform for free is because it works with Google's advertising and publisher products; they ultimately want you to see the value of investing in advertising.

To start using Google Analytics, you simply need to have a Google account and then sign up for the platform by connecting your site via a small snippet of tracking code. Shopify makes it easy to add the code; simply visit Preferences in your online store and then connect your Google Analytics account in the section marked "Google Analytics".

Another free service offered by Google, Google Search Console helps you understand how Google sees your website and then provides suggestions for how you can improve your site to boost your search engine results. Not only will it help you fix search indexing problems, but it will also show you how often your site is appearing in results and help you troubleshoot for issues, especially those related to mobile usability.

To sign up for Google Search Console and start benefitting from it, you'll need to sign up for a Search Console account, add your site and verify ownership, and then perform a quick site check-up on a monthly basis. If you don't want to learn the ins and outs of Search Console yourself, then you should consider hiring an SEO specialist.

Now that more users are browsing the web from mobile devices, page loading speed is essential, since people don't have the patience to wait for a slow site to load on a mobile phone or tablet. Google's Page Speed Insights tool provides insights about the speed of your site and then gives you tips for making the page load more quickly.

SEO

SEO is considered "organic", since you're not paying for any of the traffic it generates to your site (although you're probably paying in the time and effort required to optimize your site). With SEO, you make your website as friendly as possible for a search engine like Google, so Google will display your URL on the first page of search engine results when a user searches for a keyword related to your brand. If you want to get yourself in front of people who may not already know about your product but who are searching for products that you carry, like "pink sapphire huggie earrings", then you want to appear in the top search results.

The tricky thing about SEO is that Google doesn't want anyone to outsmart their search engine algorithm. At the end of the day, Google's main goal is to deliver the best and most relevant content to its users, so it keeps updating its criteria to prevent any one company from gaming the system. In addition, Google doesn't generally announce that it's making an algorithm update; a new update can dramatically change a website's search engine results, since the update reconsiders ranking factors.

How does Google decide that a website is worthy of getting ranked on the first page? A number of factors come into play, and they include things like content quality, content length, page load speed, mobile optimization, backlinks, image optimization, keywords in tags, keyword density, and more. No one really knows how heavily any one of these factors ranks in Google's decision-making process.

Your approach to SEO can be as simple or as complicated as you like, since there's almost always something more you can be doing to optimize your website for search. On a very basic level, you can simply make changes to "on-page SEO" (what appears on the user-facing page) by choosing some target keywords and then incorporating them into your website content in a natural way. In addition, you can start looking for press opportunities that will help other higher-authority sites link to you. Finally, you can make sure you have an SSL certificate for your site.

If you'd like to get more technical about your SEO, then you can work with an SEO specialist to address some "off-page" (backend) technical things like optimizing your site for mobile devices, increasing page load speed, optimizing your XML Sitemap, and more. Even for bigger, more established brands that already rank well for their target keywords, SEO is an ongoing endeavor, not only because Google's algorithms are frequently changing but also because search competitors are optimizing and updating their content as well. SEO is never a one-and-done solution.

Before you can begin the search engine optimization process, you'll need to first conduct an SEO competitive analysis and audit, which will help you better understand your search engine presence, illuminate the opportunities available to you in search, and demonstrate how you can improve your search engine ranking to get in front of more customers.

SEO competitive analysis and audit

I want to be clear about the fact that your SEO competitors are not necessarily your regular competitors - they're the businesses that outrank you in Google search results. For example, you may not necessarily think of Etsy as one of your competitors, but there's a good chance that Etsy is your SEO competitor, since they're probably ranking above you in Google search results for jewelry in your category.

To perform an SEO competitive analysis, you need to research the links, keywords, and content associated with your SEO competitors. Using this information, you will be able to consider how you can implement your competitors' tactics in your own SEO strategy. Instead of guessing about the best keywords for your brand, you will be able to see what's working for your competitors, so you can choose to copy them or follow a different path.

The easiest way to do an SEO competitive analysis is to invest in a search engine marketing tool like Moz or SEM Rush. First, you'll want to use the tool to find your top search competitors. For many jewelry brands, the top competitors will be the same: Etsy and Amazon almost always top the list because those sites are so massive and are already dominating search engine results. However, in your investigations, you may discover a few search competitor underdogs that are more realistic to tackle.

Once you know your competitors, you can perform a competitive keyword analysis, which will help you identify the keywords your competitors are ranking for and give you clues about keywords you should also pursue. During this process, you'll want to look for valuable keywords that you don't rank for and high-volume keywords where you rank in positions four to 15 and can potentially boost your ranking. When researching your keywords, you'll come across terms like "difficulty" and "volume"; while difficulty refers to how competitive any given keyword is, volume refers to how many people are searching for it. Ideally, you'll want to target keywords that aren't very difficult but that still get decent search volume. Finding that balance is one of the hardest parts of keyword research.

After you conduct your keyword analysis, you'll want to examine your competitors' top content: pages that have the most backlinks or links to other sites. Understanding how your competitors' content attracts interest from other sites will allow you to uncover opportunities for significantly improving upon your own content. You'll also want to see which sites have linked to your competitors and then brainstorm a list of which sites might also link to your site.

Lastly, you'll want to get inside the mind of someone who's searching for the keywords you've uncovered, since you'll want to create valuable content that matches the user's search intent. You can do that by simply Googling the keywords yourself and observing what appears in the results. Is it mostly local content? Is it very product driven? Is it more "how-to" style and informative? Use the results as a guide for your own content strategy.

SEO audit

In addition to performing an SEO competitive analysis, you'll also want to perform an SEO audit, which examines your current site performance and uncovers opportunities for how you can tweak and improve your website to rank higher in Google search engine results. To perform the SEO Audit, you'll need - at the most basic level - Google Analytics, Google Search Console, an SEO Analyzer tool like Screaming Frog, and an SEO tool like Moz or Ahrefs.

For the sake of simplicity, I'm going to stick with the bare-bones basics, because SEO audits can get very complex and technical. Overall, you'll want to look for glaring issues that may be holding you back from ranking in Google, easy-to-fix problems, and quick-win opportunities. First, you'll want to make sure that users can browse only one version of your site, since a URL can be entered in a number of different ways. For example, if you have an "https://" rather than an "http://" at the beginning of your website, you want to make sure your customers aren't accidentally visiting the wrong site by missing or adding an "s".

Next, crawling your site with Screaming Frog will help you find issues like broken links and duplicate content. You'll also want to use Screaming Frog to check your page titles and meta descriptions. These are the titles and short blurbs that accompany your URL in Google search results. While titles should be between 56-60 characters, meta descriptions should max out at 320 characters. Both should be descriptive and accurate. Ideally, you'll be using words and phrases that are relevant to your user and to the content on the page, whether it's a product or more information about your brand.

After that, you'll want to check your site speed, since that can affect your search engine rankings. Google's data shows that the longer a page takes to load, the more likely the user will abandon the page before even viewing it. If your site is not as fast as it could be, Google will provide you with recommendations for how you can improve it.

Finally, Moz or Ahrefs can help you determine the number of backlinks you have. Since Google sees backlinks as an endorsement of your site, they play a crucial role in a site's success. If you can get major sites to link to your site, then their linked endorsement will help you improve your search engine rankings.

Choosing and using keywords

In the previous section, I mentioned that an SEO competitive analysis is one way to get keyword ideas. You can also try keywords that you don't necessarily uncover by researching your search engine competitors. When brainstorming new keywords, you'll want to consider words and phrases that describe your business and products. You'll also want to brainstorm keywords that are relevant to the location of your business.

After you brainstorm a list of keywords, you'll want to use a tool like Moz or Ahrefs to check the keyword difficulty and search volume of each keyword to see if it's worth pursuing. Again, you'll want to strike a balance between low keyword difficulty and high search volume to increase your chances of ranking for any given keyword. I recommend compiling a list of at least 10 target keywords when you first begin the process of optimizing your site.

Once you've chosen your 10 keywords, you'll need to start incorporating them into your site content. You can add them to page titles, meta descriptions, product descriptions, in blog posts, in static website content, in URLs, in image file names, and more. The key is to implement them in a natural way, so they flow with your content. You may be tempted to jam all your keywords on every page of your site, but Google refers to this as "keyword stuffing" and will penalize you for doing it.

SEO "quick wins"

As you can probably tell, the ins and outs of SEO can be very complex and technical. However, you can always optimize for a few "quick wins" that should help boost your search traffic immediately.

1. Update your page titles and meta descriptions to include keywords and be more descriptive.

2. Check your images for alt tags and include keywords.

3. Sprinkle keywords into your website copy, product descriptions, and blog posts.

4. Reach out to other business owners, partners, etc. who might include a link to your site on their page. Backlinks help boost search engine visibility!

5. Start blogging regularly or update your site with fresh, new content.

6. Check for mobile friendliness and site speed (you can see these insights in Google Search Console and Page Speed Insights).

7. Look at your most highly trafficked pages in Google Analytics and see if you can mimic them by creating similar (but not duplicate) content elsewhere.

8. Optimize all your social media profiles. Consider publishing content on other platforms, like a YouTube channel or a podcast.

9. Create or update your Google My Business profile. Create or update any other relevant directory listings.

10. Write articles/guest posts for other websites. Start signing up for Help-a-Reporter-Out (HARO) emails and respond to reporters' requests for sources when relevant.

PPC search ads

Again, the acronym PPC stands for pay-per-click, which refers to the fact that an advertiser will pay a fee each time their advertisement is clicked. I sometimes joke that if you really dislike a brand, and you see one of their ads on Google, you should click it because it will charge them for that click. Usually, when a person uses the term PPC, he or she is referring to search engine advertising, more specifically to Google Ads.

Here's where lines get blurred: even though they're paid advertisements, search ads still fall under the umbrella of marketing because they're intent based. The searcher is already looking for something on Google, and the ad is simply helping that person find it. Unlike an advertisement on a platform like YouTube or Facebook, the Google Ad is not really interrupting the user's browsing and search behavior.

Theoretically, you can get faster results from a PPC campaign than from an SEO strategy, since paid advertising will give your brand exposure right away, while SEO can take weeks or even months to begin to take hold, especially if you're launching a new website. However, it's definitely not wise to focus on only PPC and not worry about SEO because PPC will only take you so far.

When setting up PPC campaigns for Google, a brand bids on keywords that are associated with the brand. For example, if the jewelry brand sells gemstone bead anklets, they can bid on that keyword for the chance to have their website show up at the top of Google Search results.

Once you choose your keywords, you'll also need to create your ads, which typically consist of a headline, your website URL, and a short description. You'll want to test different versions of the ad, so you can see which one performs best and then ultimately invest more money into the effective ad.

More often than Google Search ads, jewelry brands will want to use Google Shopping ads, which are ideal for a brand that sells products via an ecommerce store. While Search ads are text-based only, Shopping is a comparison shopping engine that allows customers to compare related products for the keyword they're searching. In Shopping ads, brands can include a product image, product title, cost, and store name; if the user ends up clicking your product image, then he or she will go directly to the product page on your website. To set up Google Shopping ads, you'll need to create a Google Ads account but also sign up for Google Merchant Center, which will require you to submit a product feed from your e-commerce site.

One advantage of Google Shopping is that it demands less work over time as compared to Google Ads. While Google Shopping requires some initial setup, after that setup period, Google will simply pull information on your product feeds to display your products in search results accordingly. However, with Google Search ads, you need to be writing copy and then constantly testing and adjusting it. In addition, Shopping ads are displayed higher on the search results page than even Search ads and definitely higher than organic search results, which then get pushed further to the bottom of the page.

According to data from Wordstream, the average cost per click for Google Shopping Ads in clothing and apparel (the closest category to jewelry) was 69 cents.[27] To get the best results from your Google Shopping ads, you'll want to optimize your product images, so they look as appealing as possible to a customer who's making a quick decision about which product to shop. For example, you can look at the product photos of your competitors and differentiate yourself by offering a slightly different product view. Like with any advertising campaign, you'll need a significant amount of money (about $300-$500 per month to start) to compete, since other jewelry brands are trying to get their products noticed too.

CHAPTER NINE

SOCIAL MEDIA MARKETING

In the early years of Facebook, only college students with valid .edu email addresses could create accounts, but only when Facebook was officially released to their school. I still remember when I was able to join Facebook: I was a sophomore at a small liberal arts college in Baltimore, Maryland, and I immediately jumped at the opportunity to join. The platform helped me expand my network at school, since I could digitally befriend my acquaintances and other people I had met casually through clubs and at events. I loved reconnecting with people from high school and my past, as soon as they were also able to get on Facebook too. I was nothing short of obsessed with social media.

From my first days on Facebook to the present, I've loved watching social media evolve: Twitter was wildly popular from around 2009 to 2012, and both Instagram and Pinterest launched in 2010. It's been amazing to witness the expansion of Facebook, which eventually acquired Instagram in 2012 and firmly established its place as a social media giant. Throughout the years, I have of course enjoyed using all these platforms, but I also interacted with them as a curious observer, trying my best to understand the psychology of the people who use social media as well as the etiquette and best practices.

Social media is definitely one thing that enabled "Web 2.0" or the social web. The advent of Facebook birthed an entirely new approach to interacting with the Internet, which is built around user-generated content, collaboration, and sharing. While Web 1.0 was about passive users consuming content, Web 2.0 is about active users contributing to the Internet and shaping it. At its heart, social media is driven by community and connection, especially when it's used with positive intentions. Of course, social media has a dark side and its downsides, but the best thing about it is that it can transcend geographical and other barriers, unite people over common interests and pursuits, expand minds, transmit news, ignite hope, inspire creativity, and help businesses grow.

Social media is ideal for sharing visual content like photos and videos, so it's perfectly suited for jewelry brands that want to show off their beautiful products. With social media, jewelry brands can attract new potential customers and build meaningful relationships with them, nurturing those customers over time and forming a bond based on trust and respect. Social media can also be used to delight customers and serve as a news platform to announce new products and promotions.

With social media marketing, you'll always want to strive to tell a new story or add to an existing one. Think of your social media feeds as a novel about your brand. Each post is a chapter or page in that novel. Your posts don't necessarily have to tell the story in any order, but each post should feel like it's part of the same novel.

To use social media strategically for your brand, you must realize that you don't have to maintain a presence on all of the platforms. Instead, you need to choose the platforms where your customers spend their time and that are best suited for communicating the story of your jewelry brand and your products. Instagram and Facebook are two of the most common social media marketing platforms for jewelry brands, and most will want to maintain a presence on both these platforms, posting once per day at a minimum. However, individual social media strategies will vary on a brand-by-brand basis.

Instagram

Founded in 2010, Instagram is based around the concept of sharing photos instantly, hence the name. During the first few years, Instagram would display photos chronologically on your feed, so you could see the latest photos your friends had shared. You could easily use hashtags to gain new followers and also find people who shared similar interests. Instagram was not flooded with brands or influencers.

Over time, businesses started to capitalize on Instagram's popularity and used it to share photos of their products. Early-adopter businesses were able to gain large followings quickly, as long as they put the time and effort into using the platform. After Facebook purchased Instagram in 2012, it started seeking new ways to monetize the platform by adding features and making changes, including video sharing in 2013, global Instagram ads in 2015, the end of chronological feeds in 2016, new business tools in 2016, and the launch of Instagram Stories in 2016.

As of 2020, Instagram is on track to reach 112.5 million U.S. users this year. The largest age category is 18-24 (75%), and 52% of users are women living in urban areas.[28] Instagram is best suited for brands with a target customer under the age of 30, but it's not necessarily a bad place for brands that cater to a 30+ customer base. Many of the people who use Instagram expect to make shopping decisions based on the content they see. Here are some interesting stats, straight from Instagram:

200 million Instagram users visit at least one business profile daily.[29]

62% of people say they have become more interested in a brand or product after seeing it in Stories.[30]

130 million Instagram users tap on shopping posts every month.[31]

To use Instagram strategically for your jewelry brand, you must make engagement a top priority. When someone likes one of your social media posts, that's a form of engagement. When someone comments on your post, that's also engagement. In general, engagement matters because it can help you get more visibility on Instagram. If you can get more people to like and comment on your posts, then Instagram will put that post in front of more people because the platform will deem it as relevant and worthy.

Overall, you'll want your posts to be engaging, and you'll want to actively engage with other users on the platform. With organic social media marketing on Instagram, you need to put in as much time and effort as you expect to get back. You can engage with prospective customers by responding to their comments or even liking and sharing their posts. In addition, you can engage strategically with other brands. As a new brand or a brand that's trying to increase engagement, how can you get more people to like and comment on your posts? It's simple but also time-consuming - you have to like and comment on other posts. I recommend setting aside about a half hour each day to like and comment on posts, but you should do it in a strategic way, engaging with relevant influencers, target customers, and brands that also cater to your target customers.

Ideal Instagram content

The types of photos and videos that do best on Instagram are clear, compelling, and unique without distractions. They pique the viewer's curiosity and stop her in her tracks. The definition of a "good" Instagram photo will vary from one jewelry brand to another, since each jewelry brand has a different look/tone/feel. Furthermore, each jewelry brand is hoping to achieve different goals with a social media marketing strategy. For example, one jewelry brand may have an edgy, alternative look and be taking steps to create brand awareness, while another jewelry brand may have a classic and refined look and be actively trying to convert their followers into customers.

Regardless, most effective and popular Instagram photos share similar qualities. These characteristics are:

The photo is unique. In a sea of photos on a typical feed, the photo is interesting enough to make the user stop and take notice.

The photo has a single dominant color, lots of background space, appropriate brightness, and minimal texture. When the user can clearly see the piece of jewelry in the photo without too much distraction, then he or she is more likely to notice and like it.

The photo follows the principles of composition: the rule of thirds, proper framing, and depth.

The photo is consistent with the jewelry brand's overall look/tone/feel, which means it contains the brand colors and effectively communicates the message the brand would like to share.

For more specific examples, you can check out the #MondayMotivation photos we post on our @joyjoyamarketing Instagram feed every Monday.

Overall, each image should contribute to your brand identity, either through color scheme or tone. Together, the Instagram feed as a whole should look coherent and attractive. The individual post matters just as much as the way all the posts work together. Include media like images with "shoppable" product tags, user-generated images from customers or influencers, up-close product photos, on-model closeups, video content, GIFs, seasonal images, quotes, lifestyle or "inspo" images related to your brand, and behind-the scenes shots. Make sure to take advantage of all of Instagram's formats and features, including carousels and product tags.

Instagram captions

You'll also want to write effective and engaging captions. Make sure that each caption is written in the tone you want to communicate. You want to inspire a feeling that supports your brand. Examples of tone include playful, serious, mature, sophisticated, earnest, eager, enthusiastic, minimalist, etc.

Alternate between short and long captions. Put the most important information at the beginning of the caption, making sure to focus on a strong and captivating opening. For example, if you're posting about a new product, you'll want to start the caption with the product name and the fact that it's new, something like "Our new Tahitian pearl bracelet...". Alternatively, you can start your caption with something catchy, memorable, and poetic. Think of the people in your life and all the different ways they speak, including the unique phrases they use in their casual speech. Similarly, each jewelry brand should have its own personality.

Regardless, most effective and popular Instagram captions share similar qualities. These characteristics are:

The caption is grammatically correct, clear, and easy to read.

The caption engages the user in some way, whether that's by educating them, inspiring their curiosity, asking them a question, or providing them with descriptive information.

The caption is consistent with the jewelry brand's overall look/tone/feel, which means it speaks in the voice the brand would use across all channels.

If a user enjoys the photo enough to not only like it but to stop and admire it for a moment, he or she will likely read the caption. The caption will provide context, reveal additional details, engage interest, explain how to buy a product, invite the user to share an opinion, or inspire the user to reveal something about him or herself. If the caption doesn't do any of those things, the user may still "like" the photo but won't feel compelled to investigate a brand further or even consider making a purchase. The best Instagram post will engage not only a user's eyes but also a user's mind and emotions.

When applicable, tag other relevant Instagram users in your captions to increase engagement. Ask questions occasionally. When possible, also include a clear call to action at the end of your caption. Invite your audience to take action in some way. Play around with emojis. Use a quote as a caption.

In addition to posting regular Instagram content, you'll also want to consider how you're contributing to your Instagram Stories, which is a type of content that "lives" for 24 hours on your profile. Stories can be posted in conjunction with a static post to promote that post further or drive traffic to the site. Stories present a unique opportunity for a jewelry brand to create more dynamic short content; the nature of Stories is less formal, so a brand can have fun with fonts and imagery without getting too caught up in production value. You can also try using Instagram Live, which will allow you to broadcast live video programming for up to an hour. Instagram is constantly adding new features and formats; by the time you read this book, you'll likely have many more options for sharing content.

Instagram hashtags

Hashtags are important because they enable you to get discovered by prospective customers. You can use up to 30 on a regular Instagram post and 10 on a Story. There are actually three categories of hashtags: Community, Branded, and Campaign. Community hashtags are most hashtags, since they represent a specific interest, niche, event, location, etc. Branded hashtags are exclusive to a brand. For example, Joy Joya uses #joyjoya on all posts. You can include your branded hashtag in your profile bio, so people know that you're using it; your fans and followers can also use the hashtag if they want to post their own photos of your jewelry. Campaign hashtags are related to a specific marketing campaign. For example, if you were working with an influencer, you might use the hashtag #InfluencerNameXYour-

BrandName to categorize all posts related to that influencer wearing your jewelry.

You'll definitely want to vary your hashtags and not use the same ones for every post. If you keep using the same hashtags, then Instagram may flag you as a spam account and "shadowban" you (true story: it happened to my personal Instagram account many years ago because I was using too many of the same food-related hashtags). When choosing hashtags, you should include a mix of some of the more popular and generic hashtags like #beauty, #inspiration, #design, and #style with some more niche hashtags. For example, if you sell pearl jewelry, then you'll want to use specific hashtags like #pearls, #pearljewelry, #jewelrydesign, and #pearllovers. Including a mix of both popular and niche hashtags will help you get seen among both general and specific audiences. The general users will boost your likes, even if those people are not qualified prospective customers. As a result, your engagement will increase. Furthermore, if you're trying to reach a niche segment of your target audience, then you can use hashtags related to that niche.

You can view the performance of your hashtags by checking out Instagram's native Post Insights. To do that, you would visit any particular post and then click "View Insights," which will appear beneath your photo in the bottom-left corner. When you expand that and scroll down to the "Discovery" section, you'll be able to see Impressions from hashtags. The number next to hashtags will give you clues about whether or not your hashtags are helping your post gain exposure.

To answer the question, "Where do I put the hashtags?", there's no right or wrong answer. You can put them immediately after the caption, you can put them after the caption with a few line breaks in between, or you can put them in the comment. Personally, I think putting them in the comment just looks nicer, but placement won't necessarily make a difference either way.

Facebook

Since Facebook owns Instagram, the two platforms share some features in common, and businesses can easily cross-post from Instagram to Facebook. However, the user demographics are slightly different. As of September 2019, Facebook has 2.5 billion monthly users.[32] 75% of women use the platform. 84% of 25–30 year olds use Facebook; 79% of 30–49 year olds use Facebook; 68% of 50–64 year olds use Facebook.[33] As you can see, the average age of Facebook users tends to be slightly older than Instagram.

In addition, people use Facebook differently, and they're not necessarily there to shop; instead, they're getting their news, connecting with friends and family, interacting with virtual communities, and generally communicating through direct messaging, groups, and more. As a result, you need to tailor your content accordingly. A business' Facebook page is more informational in nature than a business' Instagram profile, which is more about communicating a visual story. I definitely don't recommend sharing your content directly from Instagram to Facebook or simply posting the exact same caption. Instead, your Facebook posts should complement your Instagram posts but be sensitive to the differences between the two platforms.

Social media marketing is important, but you should not be overly dependent on it, since you don't own these media platforms and are at the mercy of whatever changes they make. I was an early adopter of Instagram and have seen all the ways it has changed over the years. Not only has the algorithm gotten more complex, making it more difficult for any brand to grow an organic following, but new features have been rolled out over the years: Instagram Stories, Instagram Shopping, etc. Social media marketing should play a role in any comprehensive digital marketing strategy, but it should complement other digital marketing efforts. You don't want to wake up one morning to find that Instagram and Facebook have shut down - and that they've taken all your hard-earned contacts with them.

Social proof

Few people are going to believe you or even pay attention when you share all the reasons that your jewelry is the best option in the marketplace. However, when someone who's not compensated by your jewelry brand tells other people how much she loves your jewelry, her words have more weight.

One way to boost your marketing efforts is to focus your time and attention on collecting social proof. Coined by Robert Cialdini in his 1984 book *Influence*, the term "social proof"[34] refers to a person copying the actions of others when he or she is not sure what action to take next. Consider how you've made online purchases in the past. Given the choice between two versions of the same product, both at the same price points and with the same specifications, wouldn't you choose the retailer with more positive reviews? When you're searching for products on Amazon, you may even sort by top-rated products, so you can weed out the poorly-rated options.

You may be surprised to discover that product reviews aren't the only form of social proof. Other types of social proof include expert social proof, celebrity social proof, crowd social proof, friend social proof, accolades as social proof, and customer social proof. Continue reading to find out how your jewelry brand can gain social proof in each one of these areas.

Expert social proof

One way to gain expert social proof is to be recognized by an industry expert. For example, you can try to get your jewelry featured by one or more of the most influential jewelry bloggers, like Gem Gossip, Katerina Perez, or Diamonds in the Library. In addition, you can get your jewelry examined by a top gemologist - who can provide you with quotes about your top-quality materials - or by design experts - who can comment on your innovative design.

Celebrity social proof

The most valuable form of celebrity social proof is when a celebrity simply chooses to wear your jewelry without being gifted it. However, you may also find value in the social proof you get from gifting your jewelry to a celebrity, especially is she chooses to wear it while she's out and about, being photographed by paparazzi.

Crowd social proof

The crowd is a powerful form of social proof, and today the crowd is represented by a high number of social media followers. We don't recommend you buy social media followers to provide the illusion of crowd social proof. But you should be doing everything you can to boost your social media following, since the crowd is clout.

Friend social proof

People trust recommendations from their friends and loved ones the most. Do you have a referral program in place? If you incentivize referrals, then you'll likely inspire your happy customers to tell their close friends about your jewelry. Another way to boost friend social proof is to run a social media contest that requires all entrants to tag one or more of their friends.

Accolades as social proof

Be sure you obtain any certificates and accolades relevant to the jewelry industry and your brand. For example, if you sell jewelry with GIA-certified diamonds, then you'll want to make sure that your customers know about your certification and what it means. In addition, entering – and winning – jewelry design contests is a great way to "certify" that your brand is worthy of attention.

Customer social proof

In his book *Tribes: We Need You to Lead Us*, marketing expert Seth Godin writes, "An individual artist needs only a thousand true fans in her tribe. It's enough."[35] That's right: a jewelry store or jewelry designer needs only 1,000 tried and true fans to help inspire success. How is that possible? Consider your own loyalties to your favorite brands and businesses.

For example, when you really like a local restaurant or bar, you probably tell your friends about it, and you may even invite your friends to Happy Hour or a meal. Because of you, 10 new people will learn about your favorite establishment and become fans themselves.

If you can inspire 1,000 people to become fans of your jewelry brand, those people will not only tell their friends and family members about your brand but they'll also be more likely to create content that you can share too.

Your customers are your best advocates, and you should treat them like gold. Are you encouraging your happy customers to leave reviews on Yelp or Facebook? Are you asking them to write testimonials and reviews? Are you sharing their user-generated content on your social media platforms? If not, you could be missing opportunities to boost your brand with one of the most valuable types of social proof, user-generated content.

If you have a brick-and-mortar presence, you can encourage your fans to write Yelp reviews and then borrow review highlights for your own marketing efforts. Nudging someone to write a Yelp review is as easy as sending a follow-up e-mail or making a follow-up phone call to a happy customer. Most people don't spend their days thinking about writing Yelp reviews, but a gentle reminder or even an incentive will prompt a satisfied customer to sing their praises. If you're an ecommerce-only jewelry brand, then you can cultivate the product reviews section on your ecommerce site, Etsy store, or even eBay page.

Source guest bloggers (if you already maintain a blog). Some of your fans will love the opportunity to show others how they wear or style your jewelry. Maybe these fans already have fashion blogs or Instagram accounts of their own, and they'd like to gain more followers by leveraging your blog platform. Invite your fans to contribute guest blog posts that feature their tips for wearing your jewelry.

Host a social-media-based contest that requires entrants to post something related to your brand. Maybe entrants must post a photo of themselves wearing your jewelry or submit a design idea for a future piece. Either way, they'll be entering your contest but also sharing their creativity and your brand name with all their followers.

Once you've gathered all your social proof, you'll need to share it and make sure that your prospective customers can see it. When appropriate, pull quotes from your social proof. Then, repost these quotes on your social media platforms, feature them on your blog and in your press materials, and include them in an email marketing campaign. If you have testimonials, put them on your website, and if you have video/audio social proof, be sure to include it wherever it's relevant, whether on your website, YouTube channel, or other platform. Also, consider using social proof in your ad copy.

Your supporters are worth more than what they buy from you. Their true value is in what they say about you, and you need to do everything in your power to ensure they're delighted.

Social media planning

When it comes to planning your jewelry brand's social media strategy, do you have a weekly or even monthly calendar for your posts, or are you flying by the seat of your pants? Without a plan, you could be compromising your brand identity, wasting time by brainstorming posts at the last minute, or even neglecting your social media accounts altogether while you're busy taking care of other business responsibilities. When you make a plan, you can organize your posts around promotions, holidays, new product releases, events, and anything else you'd like to share with your customers. In addition, you can ensure that you have enough content for the coming weeks and that all your content remains consistent with your look, tone, and feel.

Finding content for every day of the week on a consistent basis can start to feel like a grind, especially after many months. However, when you assign a theme to each day, you give yourself a framework for your posts. For example, you can decide that Mondays will feature fashion/lifestyle photos, while Tuesdays will feature mood photos, and Wednesdays will feature product photos. A framework can help you fill your calendar for weeks and also give you an idea of the types of content you need to generate, if you find yourself running out of fresh photos. The best part is that no one needs to know about your themes except you and your marketing team.

Another way to create structure for your social media plan is to work around major jewelry retail holidays like Mother's Day, Valentine's Day, and Black Friday, your own promotions, and special events like pop-ups. When you add these dates to a master calendar, you can see the big picture and use your social media posts to create anticipation as these dates approach. Without a master calendar in place, you'd be surprised how quickly these dates can creep up on you, passing you by with missed opportunities.

You likely browse Instagram and Facebook for fun or to spy on your competitors. Do you ever see photos and posts that inspire you, giving you ideas for future social media posts? Be sure to save them, so you're not stuck trying to remember what you saw. On Instagram, you can save your favorite posts to the default "All Posts" Collection or to customized Collections. If you prefer using Pinterest, you can screenshot photos and posts you like and then "pin" them to a private Pinterest board that you either keep to yourself or share with your marketing team.

Have you heard of apps like Planoly and Preview? These apps can help you plan your Instagram feed by allowing you to arrange your photos as they would appear on your profile. Using these apps can help you see how all your photos will work together to support your cohesive brand image. Furthermore, you can include notes about caption copy and hashtags, so you're ready to post when the date and time come. Many of these apps also allow you to share your account with your marketing team members, so everyone can get on the same page about the plan and contribute their feedback.

The pressure of the popularity contest

Did you know that anyone with as little as $3 can buy likes for Facebook, Twitter, and Instagram? These days, likes can be purchased in bulk from companies that generate very believable-looking accounts with real profile photos and descriptions. In some cases, the likes come from real people in other countries. A simple Google search and a credit card number can get you as many likes as your heart desires.

Buying likes can be tempting, especially for brands that are just beginning their social media journey and are having trouble gaining traction. Most days, social media can feel like a popularity contest. And no one can deny the theory of "social proof," which we mentioned earlier in this chapter.

If it's so easy to buy likes, why shouldn't you buy likes? Here are three reasons:

1. Social media shouldn't be a popularity contest. Instead, media like Facebook, Twitter, and Instagram should encourage engagement and interaction. And bots won't interact with brands or buy their products.

If you're an actor or model who needs to prove your "social worth" to an agent, then maybe buying likes will work in your favor: on the surface, you'll appear popular and well liked. However, if you're a brand interested in using social media to generate a loyal following, then buying likes definitely won't work for you.

2. The metric that should matter to you – your engagement rate – will suffer. Social media marketing experts don't necessarily worry about likes; they worry about ratios.

Let's pretend that you have a million followers, and 1,000 people like your photo. A thousand likes might seem impressive, but why aren't your other 999,000 followers also participating? Why aren't they liking your photo? Given the likes-to-follower ratio, 1,000 likes isn't impressive at all.

According to an article from ContentCal, "2% is seen as a good social media engagement rate on Instagram. Anything 3% or more is great."[36] You can use the following formula to determine rate of engagement:

Engagement rate = # of likes + # of comments / # of followers x 100

JEWELRY MARKETING JOY · 151

If you're buying followers, you likely won't achieve this ratio, and if you're buying likes, you'll be spending lots of money to maintain a "healthy" albeit fake rate of engagement for every post.

3. Your notifications will eventually start to annoy you. I've noticed that fake followers tend to leave spammy comments, which damage the appearance and reputation of your posts.

Social media advertising

The truth is that the only way you're going to get impressive ROI on your first social media advertising campaign is if you're extremely lucky. That's it. When it comes to advertising, you can make very educated guesses about how to build your strategy, but you'll never know for sure whether or not your advertisements will work the way you intend – until you start running them. You'll likely have to begin with a few small advertising experiments before you find an approach that works.

I want to reassure you that it's okay to not find in-stant success with digital advertising for your jewelry brand. In fact, your initial missteps and stumbles will actually benefit you in the long run. Don't get caught up in "analysis paralysis"; instead, figure out how you can move forward and gain valuable insights about your brand.

How can you make the most out of your initial baby steps into advertising? Start by running a Facebook campaign with a low daily budget, so that you can get the valuable feedback you need to move forward with a higher-budget campaign. No matter what: don't just "boost" a Facebook post or promote an Instagram post.

Why not "boost" or "promote" posts

If you "boost" or "promote" posts, you're simply wasting your money. Five dollars may not seem like a lot to waste but consider this: you could be putting that money toward a more strategic Facebook/Instagram advertising campaign that will yield results.

Let me put it this way: if you had the choice between your favorite, tried-and-true stylist for your next haircut or – for about the same amount of money – a stylist selected by a complete stranger who's never even seen a photo of you, which would you pick? Boosting your posts is like trusting your haircut to a complete stranger. Let me save you the embarrassment of walking out of the salon with a mohawk you definitely did not want.

Instead of boosting that post, consider investing in a strategic Facebook advertising campaign, which doesn't have to cost you more than $5 or even $10 per day. Not only will it be more effective, but it will also force you to sit down and think about your target audience, your brand, the way you're communicating your brand to your target audience, and your goals.

When you create a Facebook advertising campaign from scratch, you have full control over the demographic that you're targeting, which is better than blindly trusting Facebook to know who to target.

In addition, you can write interesting ad copy with a clear call-to-action, rather than simply boosting whatever you wrote on your post and hoping it resonates with your audience enough to inspire them to "Buy" or "Learn More".

Finally, you can choose images that seem popular and then test them. For example, you can try one image with two different headlines to see which one resonates best with your target audience. You may even find that your 21-30 female demographic actually isn't responding well to an image you thought they would like – and that the image is better suited for an older demographic. Advertising the right way can provide you with valuable insights about your brand.

Ad objectives

Facebook currently has 11 objectives grouped within three categories, which represent the customer journey (I'll discuss this further in Chapter 16). These 11 objectives are Brand Awareness, Reach, Traffic, Engagement, App Installs, Video Views, Lead

Generation, Messages, Conversions, Catalog Sales, and Store Visits.

When it comes to advertising your jewelry brand on Facebook, some objectives will be more helpful than others, depending on your goals and the specific thing you'd like to promote, whether that be a product, promotion, event, or something else. In general, the objectives most relevant for jewelry brands are Brand Awareness, Traffic, Lead Generation, and Conversion.

Brand awareness

Located within the category of Awareness, the Brand Awareness objective is ideal for new jewelry brands or for established jewelry brands launching new products and collections or hoping to reach customers in previously-unexplored demographics.

If you choose to advertise with the objective of Brand Awareness, you must realize that you may or may not see immediate return on your investment, since the goal of these ads is not necessarily to sell immediately. Instead, the goal is to pique curiosity among customers, invite them to get to know your brand, build trust, and become a familiar face. Typically, the call to action for brand awareness ads is to "Learn More".

Traffic

Traffic ads encourage users to go from Facebook to any URL you choose, such as your homepage or a product page. Traffic ads are ideal when used in conjunction with Brand Awareness ads, since you can retarget people who have already engaged with your brand and then send them to a specific webpage. They'll be a "warmer" audience ready to receive you.

Lead generation

Found within the category of Consideration, the Lead Generation objective is designed to attract customers who are curious enough to interact with your content – and even provide you with their email address, so you can continue communicating with them long after the ad has left their feed.

If you're a new jewelry brand, you probably don't have a very robust email marketing list. However, building that list is extremely important, so you can keep in touch with prospective customers on a regular basis and maintain more control over the way you communicate with them. Typically, the call to action for Lead Generation ads is "Sign Up", and you can encourage prospects to sign up by offering them a special discount or other perk in exchange for their email address.

Conversions

Finally, if you're eager to sell – and you're feeling confident that your brand is ready to market to potential customers this aggressively – then you're ready for the Conversions objective, located within the Conversion category. The ultimate goal of these ads is to motivate a customer to buy the product(s) featured in the ad. The call to action in these ads is almost always "Shop Now."

Once your ad is up and running, you'll want to check regularly for results. Based on the type of ad that you run and your goal for each ad, you'll be monitoring different metrics. For example, if you're running an ad with the goal of selling a specific piece of jewelry or collection, you'll want to track click-through-rate and conversions. If you're running an ad with the goal of brand awareness, you'll want to track impressions, reach, and frequency. From there, you can decide whether or not your key performance indicators or KPIs (more on this in Chapter 15) are living up to your expectations.

Facebook Pixel

One of the most exciting things about Facebook is the Pixel, a piece of tracking code that you install on your website. Facebook can tell who visits your website from the ads, and you can later retarget those people with follow-up ads. You can create retargeting ads for a warmer prospective customer, someone who decided to view your ad or go to your website but didn't make a purchase. In addition, you can even retarget with dynamic product ads, so you can show people specific products they viewed in the past. Finally, you may want to use a Conversion ad to target people even further down the funnel. Maybe those people abandoned their cart, have signed up for your email newsletter or have visited your site multiple times. You can entice those people with an ad that contains a coupon code or some other incentive to purchase.

Budget and expectations

Spending a little bit of money on these ads – even just $5 or $10 per day for two weeks – can help you determine whether or not what you think about your target customers is actually true. This valuable information can help you make better and more informed decisions about your future marketing strategy.

Another benefit of running Facebook ads is that the campaigns are in real time. You can check Business Manager multiple times per day to view how your ads are performing, and you can stop them at any time. If you invest in other forms of advertising, like a print magazine ad or event sponsorship, you may never see your ROI – or know about it for many months.

Furthermore, these ads will help you gain more mileage from your content, and you'll likely notice more potential customers liking and commenting on your posts. By exposing your brand to new people, you may even gain feedback, which can help guide future decisions about product development and more.

Running a small Facebook ad campaign can give you the confidence you need to run a more ambitious campaign down the road and to tailor your marketing strategy so that it's more effective. Even if you don't make any sales from your first advertising campaign, your investment in the ads will yield valuable data that you can analyze and then use as the basis for making important conclusions about your audience and your products.

CHAPTER TEN

INFLUENCER MARKETING

An influencer is an individual who has social influence and/or exceptional knowledge in his or her chosen field. Most of the time, we associate influencers with Instagram, but the truth is that influencers exist on many digital platforms and in real-life communities, both on micro and macro levels.

On a micro level, an influencer could be the fashion-forward small-town newscaster who's inspiring women in her community to dress and accessorize the way she does. On a macro level, an influencer could be an "it girl" supermodel who can elevate a jewelry brand from no-name to must-have in a matter of moments, simply because she's wearing a piece to a high-profile event. Influencers tend to be highly-respected early adopters who can get others to stop and take notice, usually because they're attractive and/or they possess charm and style.

Some of the most well-known fashion and style influencers today include the Kardashians, the Jenners, Alex Chung, Chiara Ferragni, Lauren Conrad, and Meghan Markle.

When it comes to social media influencers, experts have grouped them into four distinct categories, based on their follower counts: mega, macro, micro, and nano. A mega-influencer has more than one million followers, a macro-influencer has between 100K and one million followers, a micro-influencer has 1,000 to 100K followers, and a nano-influencer has fewer than 1,000 followers.

You should keep in mind that just because an influencer has more followers doesn't mean that person is a "better" influencer. In fact, most jewelry brands would be better off working with a micro or nano-influencer, depending on the marketing goals and target audience.

Is now the right time for an influencer marketing campaign?

Influencer marketing isn't for every jewelry brand. Even for the jewelry brands that could benefit from influencer marketing, it may not be an appropriate strategy at all times. The brands that benefit the most from influencer marketing are new brands hoping to gain exposure and connect with new audiences, brands that are launching new collections, brands that want to reach a target audience that engages with a specific influencer, and brands that don't have the time to wait for other types of marketing initiatives to gain traction.

However, before you move forward with an influencer marketing campaign, you must have a solid brand foundation, including a cohesive and memorable look/tone/feel, a professional and easy-to-navigate website, and attractive and regularly updated social media profiles. Furthermore, you must clearly define your target audience and create customer personas. Finally, you must have clear and measurable goals for your desired influencer marketing campaign. If you're lacking any one of these things, now may not be a great time to try influencer marketing.

What are the benefits of working with influencers?

Now that you know about the different types of influencers and whether or not influencer marketing is right for your brand, you may be feeling overwhelmed. Are you asking yourself, "What can influencers offer my jewelry brand? Is it worth the effort of working with them?"

When you find the right influencer or influencers, they can benefit your brand greatly, depending on your specific goals and target audience and how you manage your relationship with the influencer. Influencers can offer your brand five main benefits:

1. They can improve brand awareness. If you're a new jewelry brand, and you're struggling to get noticed, then an effective influencer campaign can put you on the map almost immediately. With their interest piqued, curious shoppers will want to know more about your brand, and the influencer will help drive traffic to your website or store.

2. They can help you create content. It's a proven fact that effective content marketing can attract traffic to your website or store. However, brands sometimes struggle to create and share content on a regular basis, especially when it comes to visual content. By working with an influencer, you're essentially outsourcing your content creation to that person and taking some of the burden off yourself and/or your marketing team.

3. They can help you build trust with your target audience. In today's marketplace, customers are overwhelmed by the amount of choices they have. They tend to stick with familiar ecommerce brands like Amazon and with the local mom-and-pop jewelry stores in their community or trusted jewelry store chains. Many of them are unwilling to try something new. When a trusted influencer sings his or her praises about your jewelry brand, the endorsement can immediately build trust between your brand and new customers, ultimately driving traffic to your website or store.

4. They can potentially improve your search engine ranking. Influencers can help you build links that connect back to your website and create content that you can repost on your own website and social media profiles. Both of these things can increase your legitimacy in the eyes of Google, and you'll likely see a boost in search rankings when you partner with an influencer. The more easily people can find your website, the more likely they'll be visiting your ecommerce or brick-and-mortar store.

5. They can help you gain valuable feedback about your target audience. When your influencer shares content about your jewelry brand, his or her followers will likely engage with the content, and you'll get valuable feedback. Most people will probably say things like "I love this!", but others may have critiques like "I wish this was available in rose gold." You have the opportunity to respond to all these comments and then create products that will cater to your customers' needs. When they see how responsive you are, they'll be more likely to visit your website or store.

What are the various approaches to influencer marketing?

Now that you know about the benefits of working with influencers, you're probably wondering about how influencer marketing campaigns take shape.

The truth is that there's more than one way to approach influencer marketing, and your approach will depend on your goals and your target audience. Common approaches to influencer marketing include:

1. An event marketing partnership for a brick-and-mortar store or pop-up. Will you be hosting an in-person event for your jewelry brand? One way to encourage customers to attend your event is to have a special guest: an influencer. Not only will your target customers be thrilled to meet their favorite influencer, but they'll have the chance to experience your brand in person. Even better, they'll be able to see the influencer wearing your pieces. Without the opportunity to meet this special guest, your target customers may not be motivated enough to attend the event.

2. A long-term partnership. One of the most effective approaches to influencer marketing is to establish a long-term partnership with your influencer. For this type of partnership to work successfully, the influencer should be a genuine fan and supporter of your brand because that enthusiasm and passion will shine through to target customers. A long-term partnership can be a great way to generate a steady stream of content for your social media channels and reinforce your brand image.

3. A one-time product mention or feature. Most brands use this approach, since it carries the least risk. By partnering with an influencer for a one-off campaign, brands can get the feedback they need and improve brand awareness without committing to a long-term partnership. Furthermore, the brand can define a clear end goal.

4. A collaborative partnership. With a collaborative partnership, a brand and influencer work together in a more hands-on manner. For example, an influencer might help design a product or special collection. Then, the influencer can share the new product(s) on his or her social media platforms. New customers may find your brand via this partnership.

Influencers and events

In July 2019, *National Jeweler* wrote about the bridal jewelry brand Simon G. Jewelry, which is sold by fine jewelry retailers nationwide. In an effort to support their retail partners, Simon G. hosted five key trunk show events across the country, and the brand promoted these events to potential customers by leveraging local influencers.[37]

When choosing the right influencers, Simon G. searched for fashion and lifestyle influencers who embodied luxury and expressed authenticity, "someone who would truly wear the product...not someone who just has a strong audience but is posting about lip gloss and water,"[38] according to Vice President of Marketing and Communications Brooke Brinkman. The right influencers should also have a strong following within the communities where the trunk shows would be held. Ultimately, the partnership included influencers like @oliamajd (430,000 followers), @thegrguide (17,200 followers), and @matalasi_ (13,100 followers).

To add another layer to the influencer marketing, Simon G. also used paid social media advertising. Three weeks before the trunk shows, Simon G. ran general, branded advertisements to target customers in the show cities. Two weeks before the trunk shows, the ads directed customers to stores where they could find Simon G. in their area. Finally, a week before the show, the brand promoted the specific event through the ads.

According to Brinkman, the "influencer campaign helped Simon G. show retailers the new ways consumers want to receive their information that don't involve traditional shots of jewelry pieces."[39] Simon G. considered the campaign to be a success.

Influencers and long-term partnerships

A long-term partnership is one of the most effective approaches to influencer marketing, since the influencer who agrees to this type of partnership should be a fierce and genuine supporter of the jewelry brand. Furthermore, partnering with an influencer for the long term provides a brand with lots of content to consistently add to its own website and social media feeds.

Over a series of months (or even years), the influencer in a long-term partnership with a brand will feature the brand's jewelry products, introduce new products and collections, mention seasonal promotions, help the brand gain customer feedback, and more. This influencer may also be referred to as a "brand ambassador".

An excellent example of a long-term partnership between an influencer and a jewelry brand is the partnership between Blair Eadie from Atlantic-Pacific (my favorite fashion blog) and David Yurman. For years, Blair has incorporated David Yurman jewelry into many of the outfits she shares on her blog. In one example from 2017, Blair shows how to style David Yurman's cable bracelets, which she paired with pieces from J. Crew, H&M, and Mansur Gavriel. At the end of the post, she discloses "Thank you to David Yurman for partnering on this post."[40] Over the years, David Yurman has been able to repurpose Blair's beautiful styling perspective and photos on the brand's own feeds.

Another example of a jewelry brand that partnered with an influencer on a long-term basis is Tiffany & Co., which enlisted the influence of Jack Morris (@doyoutravel) to promote some of Tiffany's more affordable products to millennials.[41]

Influencers and one-time product placements

For a one-time product placement, an influencer will showcase a piece of jewelry on his or her blog or social media feeds. These one-time campaigns work best for brands that want more social media followers, a boost in brand awareness, or the platform to promote the launch of a new product or collection. One-time campaigns can also work well for brands that are new to influencer marketing and want to test the waters before committing to a more involved, long-term campaign.

You don't have to look too hard to find many examples of jewelry brands using influencers for one-time product placements. In many cases, these influencers also wear and promote other jewelry brands, so exclusivity is not as easy to find. Mejuri, Aurate, and Zoe Chicco are three jewelry brands that regularly partner with influencers on a short-term basis.

Influencers and collaboration

The final approach to influencer marketing that I'll include here is collaboration. In a collaborative partnership, the influencer and brand work together to create something new, whether that's an exclusive, limited-edition product or a special collection. Collaborations have become extremely popular for both fashion and jewelry brands, and these days we see more jewelry brands experimenting with them.

One example of an influencer/jewelry brand collaboration is the one between stylist, writer, travel photographer, and brand consultant Lucy Williams and the jewelry brand MISSOMA. Called "1987", the collection is inspired by 80s and 90s nostalgia and Lucy's mother's jewelry box. MISSOMA describes the collection as "the ultimate jewellery mixtape" and uses the Instagram hashtag #LucyWilliamsXMissoma to promote it.[42]

A top benefit of doing a collaboration is that the influencer will also promote the jewelry pieces, so the brand gets double the marketing power. In many of her Instagram posts from the time of the collaboration, Lucy is wearing at least one piece from the 1987 collection and showing all the different ways the jewelry can be styled.

Influencer marketing is definitely one of those tactics that nearly every jewelry brand thinks they need because it's become such a marketing buzzword, especially over the past couple of years. However, I think most jewelry brands would actually benefit more from investing in tactics like content and email marketing, which can have a more lasting and long-term impact on customers. In most cases, influencer marketing is best suited for brands like Mejuri that have a large marketing budget and that aren't overly concerned about tracking the ROI of their influencer marketing spend dollar for dollar.

CHAPTER ELEVEN

EMAIL MARKETING

Email has the potential to be one of the most powerful forms of digital marketing. Not only does it get customers to stop and pay attention, but it's also proven to generate revenue for jewelry businesses. In fact, customers are more likely to pay attention to their emails than they are Instagram or Facebook, since they often already use email for work or to manage other daily communication and responsibilities.

Frankly, your customers are expecting you to email them. Research from Adobe shows that 61% of customers indicated that they prefer to receive offers via email as opposed to other channels like direct mail, a brand's mobile app, social media channels, texts, and other methods.[43] In addition, your customers want you to make it easy for them to shop by recommending products to them and informing them about the optimal times to buy.

Email addresses are like gold, since they give you access to a direct way of contacting your audience members. You have full ownership over your email list. With social media, you don't possess that same type of ownership, since platforms like Instagram and Facebook guard all user information. Just because someone is your Instagram follower doesn't mean you have permission to send that person marketing-related communications; he or she needs to opt in to your email list first.

Furthermore, you can personalize email marketing in ways that you can't personalize other content. Based on your goals, you can send emails to specific segments of your subscriber list and even automatically populate your emails with the subscriber's name and other information.

Above all, email is one of the most direct ways to communicate with your customers. With other forms of digital marketing, like social media and content marketing, you can't guarantee who will see it, but with email marketing, you have full control over the delivery. When you send an email to a subscriber on your list, you know it's being delivered to his or her inbox and that your subscribers will see your email, regardless of whether or not they choose to open it and click through the links.

So do I just draft an email and click send?

To get started with email marketing for your jewelry brand, you'll need to sign up for an email marketing platform. Personally, I recommend Mail-chimp for its ease of use and its free email marketing plan. In 2019, Shopify did cut ties with Mailchimp, and the Mailchimp app is no longer available in the Shopify marketplace. However, Shopify store own-ers can still integrate their ecommerce stores with Mailchimp by using a third-party app like ShopSync (free), Zapier, or Automate.io.

Mailchimp's Free plan includes all the basics you need to start marketing. For no money at all, you can maintain up to 2,000 contacts and send 10,000 emails per month, with a daily send limit of 2,000. To start sending emails, you don't even need to hire someone to help you, since Mailchimp's templates make it easy for you to design your email campaigns. You simply need to commit to maintaining a con-sistent email marketing calendar and sending those emails.

Before you can design and send emails on behalf of your jewelry brand, you need to build a list. You're probably thinking, "Great! I can just send emails to all my past customers and everyone I know!" Unfortunately, that's not the case. You'll need to get permission from a person before you can add him or her to your email list. Regulations for email marketing are very strict, and you'll want to adhere to best practices – to maintain your brand's solid reputation and avoid penalties. Luckily, Mail-chimp makes it easy for jewelry business owners like you to follow regulations.

Through Mailchimp, you can access sign-up forms that you can add to your website. Or, you can connect your Mailchimp account to your Shopify account – and then post a clear call-to-action pop-up or prompt on your homepage. Promote your email newsletter on your social media profiles and consider offering something in exchange for an email signup, like a discount or other promotion.

You can also send individual emails to past customers, asking them if they'd consider signing up for your email newsletter and then providing them with the link to opt in. However, you cannot simply assume those past customers would like to receive emails from you and then add them to your list.

One of the best things about Mailchimp is that the platform offers pre-built templates, so you can populate your information without having to know code. However, if you've never sent an email marketing campaign before, you may be wondering, "How should my emails look?" To jumpstart your journey, subscribe to email newsletters sent by your competitors or by brands you admire. Note how often they send their emails and observe how those emails look and feel to you.

Unless you have a plan for when and how often you'll be sending your emails, your email marketing efforts will likely get pushed aside as you tackle other priorities. Before they start working with me, most - if not all - of my clients are neglecting their email marketing campaigns, so I know from experience! You can use Google Calendar or your favorite planning system to plan your emails a month in advance. Look at upcoming holidays, your product launches, or other significant updates you'd like to communicate to your audience. Then, mark them on the calendar. That way, you'll know exactly what to send your customers - and when. I recommend sending an email at least once per week, whenever your target customers are more likely to open emails and pay attention to what you have to say. In general, the best time to send emails is in the morning, on a Tuesday or Wednesday. However, you'll need to test what works best for your brand and your audience.

Taking your email marketing to the next level

Sending basic email campaigns is fairly straightforward, but email marketing can be as sophisticated as you'd like it to be. For example, you can experiment with personalization, automation, and segmentation. You'll also want to be aware of email marketing analytics, which can help you understand how your emails are performing and what you can change in the future to boost your results.

Marketing these days is most effective when it's personalized. According to stats from Campaign Monitor, "Marketers report a 760% increase in email revenue from personalized and segmented campaigns."[44] You can include personalization in your emails. By using something called merge tags in Mailchimp or your preferred email marketing platform, you can include the person's first name in the email wherever you insert the tag. Most consumers understand that the email wasn't handwritten for them, but it's still nice to receive something with your name on it.

One of the most exciting features of email marketing is automation, which allows you to automatically send emails to customers when it matters. For example, you can email someone when they subscribe to your list, make a purchase, abandon their cart, receive their item, when they're celebrating a birthday or other milestone, and more. By using automation, you can "set and forget" your email marketing, since the emails do all the work for you in connecting with customers. When automation is done correctly, it's timed strategically and includes strong calls to action - both in the subject line and throughout the body of the email.

The only danger of automation is when the messaging feels tone deaf. During the COVID-19 pandemic, for example, you wouldn't want to automate an email to your subscribers about how they could wear your piece to an upcoming event, since most people were forced to shelter in place. You'll definitely want to check your automated emails every month or so to make sure they're still relevant and appropriate.

Thanks to email marketing segmentation, you can segment your customer list into multiple groups and then tailor your email communications accordingly. For example, if one group of customers buys from you frequently, then that group would receive one type of email, while a person who has never purchased from you would receive another type of email. Or, if someone doesn't open your emails very often, then maybe you can send that person fewer emails than the customer who always opens your emails.

Be honest: how many marketing emails do you actually open every day? You may subscribe to emails from your favorite clothing brands, entertainment venues, or local publications. But are you actually reading them? Or are you simply deleting them because you're too lazy to click "Unsubscribe"? That's how most customers feel about emails from your jewelry brand (if you're even sending emails, of course). They're suffering from something known as "email fatigue". However, all hope is not lost. Email marketing can still be effective.

To succeed with email, you simply need to know how to acknowledge that email fatigue exists and then understand how to combat it. Stop pretending that your customers are waiting with bated breath to hear from you and understand that most people don't have time to read your emails. Once you come to terms with this reality, then you can take steps to create and send emails that at least some customers may actually want to open. Even better, a few will feel inspired to take action after reading what you have to say!

Use data to email wisely

Today's major retailers send marketing emails at least once a week, if not twice a week. Sometimes, they send a daily email! If you're not a major retailer, then you shouldn't be sending emails like one.

You can still send emails that advertise your promotions for holidays, like Valentine's Day, Mother's Day, Black Friday, Christmas, etc. But before you send more than one email for any given promotion, you may want to work with an email marketing specialist, who can help you segment your lists and better understand who should receive a follow-up and who should be left alone.

Today's email marketing technologies are advanced, and you can leverage data to help you understand whether or not a customer will want to hear from you again anytime soon. Take advantage of those technologies and email wisely (and sometimes more sparingly).

If you were trying to sell a piece of jewelry to a shopper in a brick-and-mortar store, you'd approach a repeat customer differently than you would a person who's visited your store before but has never purchased anything. The same applies to email marketing. The messages you send to loyal customers should differ from the messages you send to people who have simply signed up for your email marketing list.

For example, someone who's purchased a diamond necklace may enjoy an email highlighting some of your newest diamond arrivals, so she may feel inspired to buy a complementary diamond bracelet or ring. In contrast, someone who's never made a purchase might like to receive a coupon code and more information about what sets you apart from your competitors.

Consumers are tired. Their inboxes are overflowing. They may not want to receive another email from anyone ever again. But if you approach email marketing wisely, you may be able to reach a select few at the right time, when they're itching to buy something and feeling inspired by the message you send them. Make it worth their while.

CHAPTER TWELVE

EVENT MARKETING

I wrote the first draft of this chapter before the COVID-19 pandemic, when event marketing looked much different than it does now. Before social distancing guidelines were implemented, jewelry brands could engage with customers at trunk shows, trade shows, pop-up shops, and more. In 2020, event marketing still matters, but most events are being hosted on digital platforms instead of in person. Regardless, I'll be covering both traditional and virtual events in this chapter.

Event marketing, also known as "engagement marketing" or "experiential marketing", can attract consumers to a jewelry brand and capture their attention in a sustained way. The effectiveness and importance of event marketing is impossible to deny. Younger consumers especially are drawn to brands that are investing in personalized and engaging experiences. According to research from Adobe, "Gen Z (64%) and Millennial (72%) consumers believe that brands should provide personalized experiences."[45] These younger consumers want opportunities to interact with products and enjoy immersive activities that bring a brand's story and mission to life.

The main objective of event marketing is usually to increase brand awareness. Of course, you will likely end up promoting your event to people who are already familiar with your brand. However, the energy and buzz around your event should ideally get people talking and attract new customers.

In order to be effective, event marketing must be integrated into and supported by a comprehensive marketing strategy, but it can also help you gather vital data that will enrich your other marketing efforts. In order to promote your upcoming event, you'll need to leverage other platforms. For example, if you're planning for a trunk show or styling event, you can write blog posts or social media posts about what the customer can expect when he or she attends the event. Before setting up your booth at a trade show, you can inform retailers of your presence by communicating with them via email marketing. In both instances, you'll be able to gather data about your attendees - like email address, demographics, product feedback, and more - and then use that data to make adjustments to your marketing outreach moving forward. According to research from Freeman, "88% of companies use their event marketing data to inform wider marketing strategies and make other important tactical decisions."[46] If you want to get to know your target customer more intimately, then event marketing is worth the investment.

Another important benefit of event marketing is that it can give you content to promote and share on other channels. For example, you can hire a photographer or videographer to capture content at your event and show customers trying and enjoying your jewelry. You can repurpose that content in blog posts, on your social media channels, and even in press releases to distribute to journalists. In addition, you can gather customer feedback and testimonials, which you can use on your website and in other forms of marketing content like Facebook ads. Event marketing can inspire a sense of #FOMO or "fear of missing out" in customers who weren't able to attend the event. Once they see how much fun your brand inspires, they'll want to be part of the inner circle too.

One example of a jewelry brand that has taken event marketing to the next level is the Italian luxury brand Damiani, which hosted an influencer event to celebrate the beginning of their 2017 exhibition "A Century Of Excellence And Passion", displayed at the Palazzo Reale in Milan.[47] They invited Instagram influencers like Eleonora Carisi, Paolo Stella, and Candela to dinner, where the women wore Damiani jewels and posted about the event using hashtags like #PalazzoRealeDreamsDamiani and #PalazzoRealeDreamsD. Through the Instagram photos, consumers could see the jewelry in action and enjoyed in an opulent setting where the brand intends its jewelry to be worn. Damiani sells luxury jewelry, so the goal was to create an aspirational atmosphere.

A great example of a brand that successfully hosted virtual events in 2020 is Metal & Smith. Pivoting away from their in-person trade show format in the wake of COVID-19, Metal & Smith launched its first virtual trade show in May, just in time for Mother's Day.[48] On an ongoing monthly basis, Metal & Smith gathered 30 designers to showcase on their digital platform (available to members of the trade) and on their Instagram feed. Metal & Smith senior account manager Olivia Lucas said in an article published on JCK, "virtual trade shows will become the alternative marketing tool of choice for designers",[49] especially since the future of trade shows remains highly uncertain.

Can't afford to host an event like either of these? Don't worry: you can still leverage event marketing for your jewelry brand on a smaller scale - virtually, for now, and maybe soon in person.

Trunk show or pop-up shop

For most jewelry brands without representation in a brick-and-mortar retail space, event marketing can mean a trunk show or pop-up shop. Even though you may not be able to host an in-person trunk show now, you can still plan for a virtual one - either via the Instagram Live or Zoom platforms. During the trunk show, you can showcase some of your favorite or most popular pieces, or you can curate pieces according to a theme. You can tell stories about the products and model them yourself. You'll even be able to address customer questions on the spot.

To ensure that your virtual trunk show attendees feel like true VIP customers, you can offer a special discount, only available to people who are present. The success of a virtual trunk show depends on how personal you get with your outreach. Your customers want to feel special and valued. Choose a list of your most loyal customers - or even people who regularly like and comment on your social media posts - and reach out to them individually, inviting them to your event. You'll get a much better response from your outreach efforts, and you'll take the steps necessary to win over customers for life.

While an in-person trunk show is a sales event that typically takes place in a retail boutique, a pop-up sale can happen anywhere but typically takes place in a space that's been rented for a short period of time. You may be surprised to learn that you can search for pop-up space via websites like Storefront and Popmark. Again, the success of your trunk show or pop-up shop will depend on how intentional you are with your invitations and outreach. You'll also want to focus on providing your customers with a complete experience - like offering them refresh-

186 · LARYSSA WIRSTIUK

ments, decorating the space in an attractive way, or even planning for interactive activities.

Styling event

In 2018, *JCK* published an article with the headline "Tired of Trunk Shows? Try a 'Jewelry Styling' Event".[50] With this type of event format, your jewelry brand may partner with a fashion brand and perhaps fashion stylist, hair stylist, and/or a makeup designer. Then, you can offer your customers a completely new look or makeover and make them feel more confident and empowered overall. When a customer can truly imagine herself incorporating a new piece of jewelry into her daily routine and lifestyle, she will be more likely to buy it. By providing her with all the pieces of the complete story, you help her facilitate the process. A styling event may be slightly more difficult to do virtually, but it's not impossible. You can partner with a fashion stylist or other image consultant and host a join Instagram Live or Zoom event. During the virtual event, you can offer general advice and even answer viewer questions.

Influencer event

Even if you can't host an influencer event that's as elaborate as the one Damiani hosted, you can still draw attention to your brand on a smaller scale. If you cater to a local audience, consider inviting a few local influencers to your jewelry studio or retail space for a reasonably-priced catered meal and let them try on some of your favorite pieces. During the event, take photos and share the content on your social media platforms, on your blog, and in your email marketing. Send the influencers home with bottles of wine and a small token of your appreciation. You can even do a virtual influencer event by inviting influencers to post content on their own channels and then uniting all that content with a dedicated hashtag.

Workshop or class

Do your customers tend to appreciate your jewelry more once they understand how it's made? Consider offering a master class to show your customers how you design and manufacture your product. Similar to the virtual trunk show format, you can do a demonstration via Instagram Live or Zoom. If you have the opportunity to meet your customers in an in-person setting, you can even let them try their hand at a very basic version of something you've designed to take home for themselves. Once they understand how much work and talent it takes to produce your pieces, they'll want to buy them.

VIP experience

Your most devoted customers want to feel valued, and they'd love to feel like they're part of a tribe that revolves around your brand. Since they know your brand better than anyone else, why not invite them to contribute feedback and then pamper them in return? You can consider hosting an in-person or virtual roundtable, where your VIPs get a behind-the-scenes sneak peek at you works in progress. In addition, you can ask your VIP customers what they'd like to see in future products. Reward them with an extra-special discount or a small token of appreciation.

Contest or award

Did you know that contests can be a form of event marketing? Giving something away is just a small component of a successful contest. You'll want to encourage customers to do something for you – like sign up for your email marketing list, share your content on their social media channels, contribute their ideas and feedback, use designated hashtags, or invite friends to check out products. You can also consider giving out an award to a customer who shares the best social media photo.

Like with any marketing initiative, planning and goal setting are key for effective event marketing outcomes, so you can see how well your efforts are working and gather the valuable data that will help you in your future marketing initiatives. How can you plan for experiential marketing? Follow these tips:

Set your budget

Even though event marketing can drive more business value than other marketing efforts, as I mentioned above, marketers still have trouble quantifying its value. Your first event may not result in an overwhelming increase in sales, but it will definitely boost brand awareness, as long as the event is executed correctly. You must decide how much you can afford to spend on the event, since your budget will affect the type of event you'll be able to execute.

When setting your budget, you'll want to remember that your costs will include more than just the venue, assuming you're hosting your event in a physical space. According to guidelines from Eventbrite, 43% of the budget typically goes toward marketing and promotion, 32% goes toward speakers and talent, 29% goes toward printed materials, and 18% goes toward venues.[51] Of course, this budget breakdown will vary from one brand to another, but it still provides a baseline. One advantage of virtual events is that they typically can be hosted on a budget, since you save the money on venue costs.

Create goals for your event

What are your ultimate goals for your event? Would you like to build brand awareness? Would you like to expose attendees to a new product or collection? Would you like to do market research on the people you think are your target customers? Whatever the goal, you must define it clearly and set targets.

Organize and communicate

Once you know your budget and goals, you'll need to coordinate all the logistics for putting together the event, which can either be simple and straightforward or consist of many moving parts, depending on how complex you want to get. If you have the resources, you may even want to hire an event planner to handle the communication and planning efforts or designate someone on your team to be responsible for coordinating the event.

Create a shared document or folder – like a Google Sheet, Google Doc, or Dropbox folder – and share it with all the event stakeholders. This central document should include every piece of information, including event timeline, costs, vendor contracts, a contact log, to-do list, attendee information, etc.

You'd be surprised how many minor details are involved in the execution of one event. For example, if you decide to move forward with a trunk show in a clothing boutique, then you'd have to coordinate the logistics with the shop owner and any employees who will be working the trunk show. If you're going to be serving appetizers alongside your jewelry, you'll want to iron out the details with your caterer. Finally, if you're going to hire a professional photographer or videographer to capture marketing content (I highly recommend this, so you can have lots of social media content), you'll want to set clear expectations.

Promote the event

The only way to attract the right people to your event is to promote it to your target customers early and often, and the best method for promoting your event is to incorporate promotional content into your regular overall marketing strategy.

As a general rule, you should start promoting your event three to four months in advance, but some smaller events may only need about a month of promotion time. Some virtual events will likely only require one to two weeks of promotion time. Look at your upcoming content calendar, including your social media posts and blog posts if relevant, and decide how you can intersperse news about your event into your regularly-scheduled content. If you don't already have a content schedule, then hosting an event can be a great motivator for you to understand the importance of a marketing/content calendar and to fully embrace it.

Facebook advertising is excellent for event promotion, since you can turn an event listing into an advertisement and expose it to a very specific target demographic. Email marketing is also an excellent tool for promoting your event, since you can personalize your email communications and create tailored event invitations. Finally, you can use social media platforms like Instagram Stories to engage your followers and pique their interest in your event.

Gather data and measure results

Event marketing presents a major opportunity for interacting directly with your customers and asking them about the customer experience, how they feel about your brand and products, and what they'd like to see in the future. Events allow you to understand your customers more intimately.

After you execute your wildly successful event, you'll want to measure your results. When it comes to event marketing, the most commonly tracked metrics include number of attendees, brand awareness, social media mentions, and amount of sales generated. Ultimately, the results you measure will vary depending on your original goals.

CREATING MARKETING HARMONY

CHAPTER THIRTEEN

GOALS, STRATEGIES, AND PLANS

Jewelry entrepreneurs often use the terms "marketing strategy" and "marketing plan" interchangeably, but the two things are actually not the same. When you first launched your jewelry business, you may have put together a business plan, which would serve as the roadmap for your business. It probably included elements like a company overview, some information about your business model and products, information about the people involved in your business, and more. You may have even included a section about your approach to marketing and sales.

When was the last time you revisited your business plan and your section about marketing in particular? In 2019, 50% of business owners did not establish any marketing goals, according to the results of a report from Outbound Engine. In addition, 50% of those surveyed did not have a marketing plan for the year, and 58% only spent five hours or fewer on marketing each week.[52] If you don't have a marketing strategy and plan, then your business is probably lacking direction and vision.

Marketing strategy

A marketing strategy basically describes the "why" and "what" of your marketing. In a larger organization, the marketing strategy would be handled by the chief marketing officer or CMO. In a small business, the business owner - working alongside a marketing consultant - would be very closely involved in the development of the marketing strategy. Overall, a marketing strategy should unite everyone on your team, especially anyone who's involved in marketing decision-making or execution.

Typically, a marketing strategy establishes your big-picture goals, so it will run parallel to your overall business strategy, mission statement, and brand identity and values. It may change and evolve over time but should not change as much as the plan, since a strategy ultimately describes what you want to achieve and aligns your marketing vision with your long-term business goals. If you make a major business decision like changing your pricing, then you'll want your marketing strategy to support the new business goal.

The elements of a marketing strategy will vary from one business to another, but typically a strategy includes a competitive analysis, customer personas, your marketing budget, your unique selling proposition, an audit of your brand's strengths and weaknesses, your goals, and your marketing mix (all the channels, platforms, and tactics you'll be using for your marketing).

Marketing plan

In contrast, your marketing plan is the "how" of your marketing. In most organizations, the marketing plan is handled by a marketing manager, who oversees all the moving parts of the plan. A marketing consultant can also help a small business owner devise the appropriate roadmap.

The plan is usually a short-term, tactical guide that describes the campaigns you'll be implementing to support your marketing strategy, and it should be specific and measurable. For example, your plan may involve a six-month timeline and include details about how you'll be handling your social media posts and on which platforms, or it could involve a year-long timeline and include details about your approach to email marketing.

A marketing plan will vary greatly based on your individual marketing initiative, but in general it should specify your tactics, the channels and tools you'll need, any collaborators or stakeholders, your budget, your key performance indicators, the metrics you'll be using to track your success, and your timeline.

No matter what, you'll need both a marketing strategy and a marketing plan for your jewelry business because you can't execute the "how" of your marketing without knowing the "what", and you won't get anywhere with your "what" unless you also have a "how".

Making the most of your strategy and plan

To make the most of your marketing strategy and plan, you'll want to get used to setting SMART marketing goals. The acronym SMART was first coined in 1981 by George T. Doran, a consultant and former director of corporate planning for Washington Water Power Company. In a paper titled "There's a S.M.A.R.T. Way to Write Management's Goals and Objectives",[53] he designated five key adjectives that should always be associated with a SMART goal: specific, measurable, attainable, relevant, and time-based.

To set your SMART marketing goal, you'll want to be **Specific** about what you want to accomplish, determine how you'll want to **Measure** and assess your progress, keep the goal **Attainable**, make the goal **Relevant** to your overall business goals and target customer, and ensure the goal is **Time-Based**. Some examples of SMART jewelry marketing goals include:

"Within the next six months, we'd like to grow our email marketing list by 25% in order to maintain relationships with new customers and inform them of upcoming promotions."

"Within the next three months, we'd like to add 1,000 new followers to our Instagram account, since most of our website referrals have been coming from the social media platform."

Specific

When a goal is specific, it will have an entire action plan attached to it, so you'll know exactly how to steer the course in order to move forward. Nonspecific goals are the types of goals that fill our daydreams and fantasies, while specific goals are the ones that actually inspire us to put pen to paper and set deadlines and priorities. When you're specific, you approach your goal setting like a journalist and answer the 5Ws: who, what, where, when, and why. Furthermore, even someone who's not familiar with your jewelry business should be able to understand your goal, since it's so specific and detailed.

Measurable

If you're not choosing key performance indicators and analyzing your campaigns, then you're basically wasting your marketing efforts and dollars. Marketing without measurement is like throwing darts at a dartboard while wearing a blindfold.

A key performance indicator, or KPI, is a type of performance measurement that can help you better understand the effectiveness of your marketing efforts. To choose the right KPIs for your jewelry marketing, you must have clear and specific goals in place and a plan for achieving those goals. I'll share more information about KPIs in Chapter 15.

Attainable

Why would you set yourself up for failure? Sadly, many people do set themselves up for failure during the goal-setting process because they're too idealistic, they underestimate the amount of work it will take to achieve the goal, or they're not fully committed to achieving the goal - and are seeking an easy excuse. In order to make a goal attainable, you may have to overcome long-held negative beliefs, develop a new skill or two, or hire someone to help you. Before you commit to the goal, make sure that you have the time, energy, and resources to realistically achieve it.

Relevant

Before you commit to any one goal, ask yourself, "What does this goal mean to me? How will it help me take my business to the next level?" If it's unclear exactly how achieving the goal will help your business grow, then you may want to reconsider why you're doing it. Is the goal you've set just a distraction from a real goal that you should be pursuing instead? Are you simply checking off the boxes instead of uncovering the goals that are most valuable to your business? Be honest with yourself about what will and won't matter in the long run. Just because another jewelry business is pursuing a goal doesn't mean it's right for you.

Setting relevant goals will help you avoid "checklist marketing", a term coined by author Nick Westergaard in his book *Get Scrappy*.[54] He uses this term to describe a very common yet misguided approach to marketing: far too many business owners skip the SMART goal-setting process, so they're clueless about what they want their marketing to achieve and disappointed when their marketing doesn't achieve it. Instead, they experiment with every digital marketing tactic under the sun and then go through the motions with their marketing efforts, copying their competitors' approach to marketing or fulfilling what they believe are today's best practices in marketing. Then, they wonder why they aren't seeing results and often blame others for their shortcomings. They'll say things like, "The new Instagram algorithm sucks!" or "The influencer marketing agency screwed me over." Checklist marketing is a dangerous and - frankly lazy - attitude that provides you with the illusion that you're doing all the right things.

If you feel completely overwhelmed by all your current and planned marketing initiatives or feel pressure to "do" more marketing, just to keep up with your competitors and your head above water, then you may be guilty of checklist marketing. Instead of thinking strategically about where to invest your time, effort, and money, you try to do everything all at once. I want to let you in on a secret: you actually don't have to be on every digital marketing platform to achieve success. I promise! I'm giving you permission right now to drop some of the marketing platforms that aren't yielding any results or helping you communicate your brand, so you can take the time to focus on the marketing platforms that do.

Time-based

Do you ever mean to get something done and then end up putting it off indefinitely because you never held yourself accountable to complete it? When you make your goal time-based, then you assign a timeline to achieving it, so you know when you're staying on track and when you're veering off course. If you don't have a timeline, then you will never know when to pivot or double down any time unanticipated challenges arise. In addition, you'll never be able to assess your progress or measure success if you're not sure when you should have reached certain milestones.

In your head, you probably already know exactly what you'd like your marketing to achieve. However, if you don't commit your strategy to paper (or a digital document), then you'll never be able to share it with anyone, and you may forget some important aspects. According to data from CoSchedule, "marketers who document their marketing strategy are 538% more likely to report success than those who don't".[55] Even if you're just beginning your journey as a jewelry business owner, and you're not sure about your strategy, you must document it. Take action; don't let "analysis paralysis" hold you back from laying the foundation for your marketing strategy. Of course, you'll also want to record your plan, so that every person who's involved in executing it knows what to do and what's expected. Even if you're the only person creating and executing the marketing plan, you need a guide that will keep you accountable and on track.

CHAPTER FOURTEEN

BUDGETING AND ROI

Marketing your jewelry brand takes time, effort, persistence, consistency, resources, and faith. If becoming the next Tiffany & Co. is as easy as starting an Instagram account and posting a few photos of your jewelry, then every jewelry business would be wildly successful, and none of them would need marketing professionals.

If you don't set appropriate expectations about your marketing efforts, then you may only view the results through a certain lens. When you're single-mindedly focused on achieving a specific goal or realizing a certain outcome, then you may not be able to "see the forest for the trees", as they say. Instead, you'll blind yourself to new possibilities and close your mind to happy accidents and new ideas. You'll also miss the fact that no marketing campaign executed correctly will ever be a waste of time because the valuable data and feedback can inform your decisions moving forward.

One of the easiest and most efficient ways to set your expectations is to study what other jewelry brands have been able to achieve through their marketing efforts. A great way to keep your finger on the pulse of industry news is to regularly read publications like *JCK*, *INSTORE*, *WWD*, *Retail Dive*, *National Retail Federation*, *AdWeek*, *AdAge*, and *Marketing Dive*. Once you see that even major jewelry brands are constantly reinventing themselves and sometimes failing at marketing, then you'll better understand that marketing is a process - definitely more of an art than an exact science.

How much can you expect to pay for various types of marketing services when enlisting the services of an outside consultant or agency? Please consider the following as general guidance only, since prices for marketing services can vary based on many factors, including your geographical location, your individual goals, the amount of work that needs to be done, consultant/agency experience, and more. However, if you encounter a service that costs significantly less or significantly more than the ranges I provide here, then you should be wary and move forward with caution. In those cases, the service provider may be inexperienced or unqualified, or they could be trying to swindle you.

You should also know that you can probably outsource many of these marketing services to an overseas freelancer, who can perform the work at low cost. However, before you decide to do that, consider the possible stress of overcoming language barriers and cultural differences. Furthermore, the very nature of freelance work means the contractor is likely delivering your finished product on a piecemeal, as-needed basis, so that person will never have the chance to become intimately familiar with your brand. As a result, the deliverables may be inconsistent and require multiple revisions; the quality may suffer. Developing a long-term relationship with a consultant or agency who can invest the time, effort, and expertise in your brand will help you ensure that the job gets done right the first time and that the work is consistent with the professional image you want to present to your customers.

Below, you'll find approximate pricing for content marketing, search marketing, social media marketing and advertising, influencer marketing, email marketing, event marketing, branding, and ecommerce optimization, all common marketing services that today's jewelry brands need.

Content marketing

Content marketing involves two major components: content strategy and content creation. To hire a professional who can create a content strategy, you should expect to pay a one-time fee of $500 to a few-thousand dollars, depending on how many channels you're using and how multifaceted the strategy will be. For written content like blog posts, which would be created to support your content strategy, you can expect to pay between $150 to $700 per piece, depending on the word count, the amount of SEO optimization desired, the amount of research involved, and more. Of course, you can always source cheap content from sites like Fiverr, but the result will probably also look cheap. If you're thinking about adding video to your content marketing mix, you can expect to pay between $1,000 and $3,000 per finished minute when working with a semi-professional video production company. Yes, video is expensive!

Search marketing

How much should you be paying for assistance with search engine optimization? You can definitely get started on your own for free by executing some quick wins. Paid tools like Moz and SEMRush, which can support and streamline your search engine optimization efforts, cost between $79/month and $400+/month. Hiring a consultant or an agency will cost between $500 and $5,000 per month depending on the scope of work. The process of optimizing a website for search engines involves many moving parts, so you'll want to get crystal clear on what the agency is promising before you agree to any service offerings or packages.

Social media marketing and advertising

Of course, social media marketing can cost noth-ing (excluding your time) if you do it all yourself. However, you're probably going to have to spend some money on high-quality product and lifestyle photography. Hiring an agency to handle your social media marketing can cost as little as $500/mo. for very basic planning and posting on one platform like Instagram (with little-to-no original content crea-tion, so you would need to provide all the content) and can cost up to $4,000 for very comprehensive management. On the high end, a consultant or agen-cy would be managing multiple social media platforms, developing a strategy with a plan and goals, creating and posting original content accord-ing to the strategy, monitoring KPIs, interacting and engaging with potential customers, and more.

In addition to organic social media marketing, you may want to add paid social media advertising cam-paigns to your marketing mix. I highly recommend hiring a professional to handle social media advertis-ing for you, since setting up and executing successful advertising campaigns take skill and expertise. In addition, since you'll be spending money on the ads, you'll want to feel confident that your money is be-ing spent efficiently. To be frank, advertising platforms like Facebook Business Manager and Google Ads are not very intuitive to use; all the cli-ents I know who have tried navigating these platforms themselves end up feeling very frustrated and defeated. They may be able to figure out how to initially set up the campaign, but they're ever quite sure they've done it correctly or are spending their money the right way. Furthermore, they may not understand how to interpret the results.

Without factoring in the actual advertising budget, a consultant or agency will cost you an initial setup and then a monthly maintenance fee that's usually a percentage of the monthly ad spend. The setup fee can be between $250 and $1,000. Typically, when it comes to brands with larger advertising budgets, an agency will charge a maintenance fee that amounts to 10-20% of the monthly ad budget. Or they may opt to charge a set monthly retainer or flat fee. For the ads themselves, my small business clients usually invest about $200 and $500 per month. However, some Facebook ad experts will argue that you need to spend a few thousand per month on ads to get the data you need to iterate effectively and to see any results.

Influencer marketing

A number of factors will impact how much an influencer charges for his or her services: follower count, reach and engagement, how you'd like the influencer to feature your product, the amount of work involved, the number of channels being used, and more. In addition, if you're communicating with the influencer via an agency, then that agency will also charge a premium. To give you a general idea, mid-tier Instagram influencers (with 50,000– 500,000 followers) typically charge $500 to $5,000 for a single Instagram post. For more specific information and to learn more about the going rates for influencer marketing and various platforms, check out a regularly-updated resource like Influencer Marketing Hub or reach out to some influencers yourself - most would be happy to send you information about their pricing.

Email marketing

The cost of email marketing depends on factors like: how many subscribers you have, how often you send emails, your email marketing goals, and more. First, you'll need to consider the operating costs of your email marketing platform. For example, Mailchimp offers a free plan that allows you to maintain 2,000 contacts on one list. After you exceed 2,000 contacts, the pricing ranges from $9.99/month to $299/month. Working with a consultant or agency to help you manage and execute your comprehensive email marketing strategy can cost you $500 per month or more, depending on how frequently you email your subscribers and how sophisticated you want to get with tactics like automation, personalization, and segmentation.

212 · LARYSSA WIRSTIUK

Event marketing

Of all the services on this list, event marketing varies the most, since events can be scaled from very small and intimate with mostly DIY elements to very large and elaborate. Furthermore, most events are now being held virtually, so the cost of a physical location is no longer a variable. Instead, brands need to worry about costs associated with technology and paid social media promotion. Theoretically, virtual events can be executed for free, minus any costs to promote the event. Professionally produced in-person events can cost as little $5,000 and be as expensive as a few hundred thousand dollars.

Branding

Working with a graphic designer to refine your branding definitely requires a significant investment, but your brand is a long-term commitment that can make or break your business. An original logo will cost between $750 and $5,000. A complete brand identity and style guide will cost you $3,000 on the low end but can cost as high as $20,000 depending on the designer's experience and level of involvement. Most independent graphic designers I know will charge between $3,000 and $6,000 for the following comprehensive branding services: brand kickoff workshop, mood board presentation, branding directions/brand system, and a brand style guide.

Ecommerce optimization

How much can you expect to pay a professional to set up your ecommerce website? First, you'll have to consider the technology costs. A platform like Shopify will cost you $29/month on the low end and $299/month on the high end. Website hosting will cost about $5/mo. If you purchase a pre-built premium Shopify theme, that theme will cost you approximately $180, but you'll likely have to customize it to make it work for your brand. You can hire a developer to customize the pre-built Shopify theme for a few hundred to a few thousand dollars, depending on the complexity of your requirements. For a completely customized Shopify store, you can expect to pay a design agency between $5,000 and $20,000+.

Setting a budget

You may have heard the phrase "You have to spend money to make money", and that definitely applies to jewelry brands that want to increase market share and remain competitive in their respective categories. How much should you be spending on marketing your jewelry brand every year, and how should you be distributing that marketing budget across multiple marketing channels?

Many jewelry entrepreneurs struggle to understand how much they should be setting aside for marketing, especially if they're growing a new business and trying to increase brand awareness without any idea of how much revenue they'll be making. To make matters more complicated, a jewelry business can determine its marketing budget in a number of different ways, and unfortunately no one-size-fits-all formula or solution exists.

What you'll need to know first

Before you can determine your marketing budget, you'll need to consider a number of factors. First, you'll need to understand that how long you've been in business will affect your marketing spend. Are you a new company that desperately needs brand awareness, or are you a more established company that simply wants to stay top-of-mind with its audience? As a general rule, a newer jewelry brand will need to spend more on marketing than a well-known brand. Furthermore, your marketing spend may vary based on your business model. For example, B2C jewelry companies generally spend more on marketing than B2B jewelry companies. After you gauge your needs based on your current position in the marketplace and your business model, you'll also want to calculate your gross revenue, which is the revenue your company receives before taxes or any other deductions. In some instances, your marketing budget will simply be a percentage of the gross revenue; in other instances, it will serve as a guide to help you set appropriate marketing goals.

Start-up jewelry business

If you're a brand-new jewelry business without any sales history, then you may not even know your revenue. According to the U.S. Small Business Administration, businesses during the brand-building years spend much more than established businesses on marketing - up to 20% of their anticipated gross revenue[56]. You're probably wondering, "Where am I supposed to get the money if I'm not making any money?"

In some rare cases, a jewelry brand is able to receive outside funding, which they can use to support their marketing efforts. For example, the jewelry brand Mejuri raised $30 million in Series B funding in 2019, bringing the total investment in the company up to $38 million.[57] It's not clear what percentage of those funds is used for marketing, but they've been able to invest some of that money in lucrative marketing efforts like influencer marketing, paid social media marketing campaigns, professional product and lifestyle photography, and more. As a result, they've been able to grow at a rapid-fire pace.

If you're not Mejuri, then you're like most brand-new jewelry brands, and you need to establish a fixed marketing budget, which means you simply have to choose a number you feel comfortable spending and then scale from there. Regardless of the number you choose, you must commit that number to paper and then do your research to figure out how to maximize your spend, so you can eventually increase your marketing budget in a strategic way.

Other new-to-market small business owners determine their marketing budget based on their short-term objectives. For example, if they know that a certain amount of money will help them promote their virtual trade show event, which will likely help them reach a monetary sales goal, then they will decide they feel comfortable spending that amount, since they feel confident they will profit from their one-time marketing investment. I tend to discourage this fly-by-the-seat-of-your-pants approach, since it doesn't really support long-term planning, but it does work for "scrappy" new brands that are trying to make money they can reinvest into a more sustainable, long-term marketing budget.

Established jewelry business

If you run an established jewelry business with a fairly predictable annual revenue, then you have an advantage when it comes to planning your marketing budget. The SBA asserts that established small businesses with revenues less than $5 million should be dedicating 7 to 8% of their revenue to marketing and then distributing that budget across brand development and advertising costs.[58] Brand development may refer to upgrading your ecommerce website, creating content for your blog and social media channels, updating your marketing videos, and more. Advertising costs may refer to the cost of Facebook or Google ads and the fee to have a professional manage those ads for you. These costs should also cover any tools or technologies you use to support your marketing efforts like your email marketing provider, your website hosting costs, your social media planning tools, and more.

These guidelines from the SBA assume that your business has profit margins in the range of 10 to 12%.[59] To put that range into perspective, most fine jewelry brands far exceed that margin. One study from *INSTORE* in 2018 showed that the average profit margin for jewelry brands is about 45%.[60] Of course, the profit margin will vary based on your product category and specific business model. If you're operating at a loss, then you should not use the SBA's budgeting guidelines for your business. Instead, you should first focus on lowering your margins and spending more on marketing, so you can start making sales - and get out of the "red".

Instead of following the percentage approach, some jewelry business owners simply try to determine how much their competitors are spending on marketing and then try to match that in an effort to "keep up with the Joneses" and not fall behind.

Distributing and updating your budget

To distribute your marketing budget, you'll also want to consider all the ways you'll be marketing throughout the year, which should be outlined in your marketing plan. Your chosen channels and tactics can include your social media presence, your email marketing campaigns, your photography, your digital advertising, your website, your SEO, and more. While it's true that some of these things can be managed for free - like social media and SEO - you'll still need to consider your time, any paid tools that are helping you optimize your processes, and any consulting fees you incur from professionals outside of your organization.

You should also know that your marketing budget isn't necessarily fixed. For example, during the COVID-19 pandemic, many jewelry entrepreneurs cut back on their marketing budgets because they lost revenue or were feeling uncertain about the future. On the other hand, some jewelry entrepreneurs actually doubled down on their marketing spend during the COVID-19 pandemic because they realized they could increase market share while their competitors weren't spending as much money on marketing.

Strategic spending

Knowing how much to spend on marketing is just a small part of using your marketing budget effectively. In addition, you'll want to spend that money in a strategic, thoughtful way and put it toward initiatives with the best return on investment. You'll need to have both a sound marketing strategy and plan, and you'll need to understand both your competitors and your customers. Even though hiring an experienced marketing consultant can eat into your marketing budget, that person's knowledge and wisdom can help you save money in the long run because he or she can advise you on the best decisions for your brand.

Unfortunately, some jewelry business owners don't understand the value of high-quality marketing, and they try to cut corners by hiring cheap service providers. However, "You don't always get what you pay for, but you always pay for what you get", as the saying goes. If you don't spend your marketing budget wisely the first time, you'll probably have to spend it again - and again.

Taking the time to track your marketing results and measuring the efficacy of your marketing will also help you understand the true value of your marketing budget. If you experience a stellar sales month, then you may want to evaluate what you did differently that month - and then invest more money into whatever that may be. If you had a dismal sales month, then you may want to pull back on the type of marketing that you were doing that month. At the same time, you do need to realize that your sales results aren't necessarily a direct result of your marketing, since market fluctuations can also happen for other reasons. In addition, you should know that the results of some marketing tactics - especially influencer marketing - can be difficult to measure, so you have to feel comfortable with a small degree of uncertainty about your marketing spend. All in all, as long as you're following a plan and making conservative decisions based on your business goals and realistic expectations, then you're more than likely choosing the right marketing budget for your jewelry brand's current situation.

Return on investment or ROI

Today's jewelry business owners want to see exactly how their marketing dollars are working for them. However, marketing is complex, since it targets consumers at all stages of the buying process, and return on investment - or ROI - is sometimes difficult to measure, especially in the digital world. ROI is the difference between the amount of money you spent on a marketing campaign and the revenue you made as a result of that campaign. Unfortunately, a universally "good" ROI doesn't exist, since every jewelry brand has its own ideas about ROI. Unique factors like goals, investment, specific campaign tactics, campaign duration, and more can all influence ROI. For example, your target ROI for your latest email marketing campaign may be different for your benchmark ROI for your Facebook advertising efforts. To make matters even more complicated, monetary ROI isn't always the ultimate goal of any given marketing campaign. Sometimes, you may be more focused on increasing brand awareness, so new subscribers to your email list would indicate positive growth. The more marketing you do for your jewelry brand, the more realistic you'll be about ROI, especially when you see what is - and isn't - possible. Moving forward, you can use your past results as benchmarks and then challenge yourself to do better next time.

CHAPTER FIFTEEN

MEASURING RESULTS

Key performance indicators, also known as KPIs, are measurable values that can help you understand whether or not you're on track to reach your goals. Instead of guessing about the results of your marketing efforts, you can use KPIs as your guideposts; they will alert you about when to pivot, when to double down on your efforts, and when to move forward steadily. They should be assessed at consistent and regular intervals.

The KPIs used most commonly by ecommerce jewelry brands measure activity related to consumer shopping behaviors, email marketing success, social media activity, and more. They include website traffic, social media reach and engagement, ecommerce conversion rate, search engine visibility, and email click-through rate.

Website traffic

If you exclusively sell your jewelry on your website, and you suspect that no one's actually coming to your website, then you obviously have a problem. You can't set goals or create a strategy for increasing your website traffic if you aren't aware of your current traffic volume or what you'd like it to be in the future. If you're not already monitoring your site using Google Analytics, then you need to connect your website to this indispensable free tool, which can help you better understand changes in your traffic.

With Google Analytics, you'll not only be able to notice changes in your website traffic, but you'll also be able to monitor other KPIs like new visitors vs. returning visitors, time on site, bounce rate, and more. Tracking website traffic is especially important during the growth phase of your jewelry business, when you're simply trying to do everything you can to get more potential customers to visit your website. As time passes, you may want to get more specific with your website monitoring KPIs and enable advanced analytics like funnels and content groups.

Social media reach and engagement

Most jewelry brands that use social media marketing to promote their businesses have noticed that organic reach is not what it used to be, especially when it comes to Instagram and Facebook. Organic reach refers to the number of people seeing your posts when you're not paying for ads.

One article from SocialInsight.io even predicts that businesses will soon have zero organic reach because Facebook and Instagram "don't want you to be able to reach your target market without paying to reach it."[61] However, before that time comes, you should still be aware of your reach because it's an important KPI no matter what you're trying to achieve with your social media marketing strategy.

While you're moving forward with social media marketing, you'll also likely want to measure your engagement, since engagement can shed light on how many people are actively interacting with your posts, rather than simply "liking" them. Engagement refers to the number of people interacting with your posts: the likes, comments, and shares. Other social media KPIs include follower or fan count, total likes, average likes, click-through rate, and more. To measure these KPIs, you'll want to use Facebook and Instagram's native insights or Iconosquare, which is a third-party social media analytics tool.

Ecommerce conversion rate

If you've already moved beyond the growth phase of your jewelry brand, and you're implementing marketing strategies to increase your sales, then you must be aware of your ecommerce conversion rate. This KPI tracks how many people make a purchase after visiting your website. Once you know your conversion rate, you can take appropriate steps to increase conversions, like improving your site navigation, adding incentives like coupon codes, and including robust product information along with beautiful and clear product photography. To track conversion rate, you can use Google Analytics, and you can dig even deeper into ecommerce conversion with KPIs like shopping cart abandonment.

Search engine visibility

Are your target customers finding your website? If your website isn't ranking on the first page of Google search results for your targeted keywords, then you may never get seen. Search engine visibility refers to how well your website is ranking in search results across the keywords you're tracking. For example, if you want your site to be ranked for "diamond engagement rings", then search engine visibility will help you understand how you rank for that keyword term. This KPI is especially important for new brands hoping to be discovered by customers, and to track this KPI you'll need to use a paid tool like Moz or Ahrefs or consult with a search engine marketing consultant.

Email click-through rate

If you actively send email marketing campaigns to your customers, then you'll likely want to track click-through rate, especially since the goal of most emails is to get your prospective customers off the email and onto your site, where they'll hopefully make a purchase. Of course, you could also measure other KPIs like unsubscribe rate, open rate, and subscriber growth rate. However, click-through rate is very useful if you're focused specifically on conversions.

To measure click-through rate, you could use the built-in analytics provided by your email marketing platform, like Mailchimp. Or, you could add a UTM parameter to the links you want to track in your email. From there, you could check Google Analytics to see how many people visited your website by clicking through the email.

These five KPIs represent a very small sampling of all the ways you can measure and track your marketing performance and progress, and they by no means represent all the ways you can and should be evaluating your data. In fact, depending on your goals, these KPIs may not even be relevant to your jewelry brand at the present moment. While some KPIs are more useful for short-term marketing campaigns, others are essential for long-term marketing efforts – but the truth is that no two jewelry brands will need all the same KPIs at the same time.

Choosing the right KPIs is a highly individualized process that can change and evolve over time for your jewelry brand. An experienced and knowledgeable marketing consultant can not only help you identify the right KPIs but also point you to industry benchmarks, so you know what to expect from your results and understand how to interpret your data.

UNITING MARKETING AND SALES

CHAPTER SIXTEEN

THE CUSTOMER JOURNEY

"Your brand is not for everyone. It isn't.
It's for the people who want something you can
help them get, who value the same things you do,
and who see the world the same way you do.
And that's not everyone."
Tamsen Webster

The customer journey is a roadmap that helps you understand all the ways that a customer interacts with your brand before making a purchase - and then even after the purchase. For example, in the first step of a journey, your customer may learn about your brand through a Facebook ad. Next, she may see your jewelry on a celebrity influencer. After that, your customer may feel curious enough about your jewelry to search for your brand on Google and then browse your website. Not yet ready to buy but intrigued by your products, she may sign up for your email updates. Your customer receives your emails for a few weeks before deciding it's finally time to treat herself to something new - a ring. Plus, you just offered a coupon code that entices your customer to take action. After she makes the purchase and receives the ring, she shows it off to her friends, who decide to follow your brand on social media. She may also post about her new ring on her own Instagram feed. In summary, the customer journey refers to every interaction a customer has with your brand.

The marketing funnel

A marketing funnel can be used alongside a customer journey roadmap, but the funnel actually refers to something a little more abstract. The customer journey is about the customer's physical touchpoints, and the funnel is about the customer's mentality, which has some relationship with the customer journey but does not always directly correlate.

In marketing, a funnel refers to the steps you'll need to take in order to nurture your prospective customers, so they can eventually become life-long fans of your jewelry brand. To put it simply, the funnel describes the customer's mindset from awareness to purchase.

If you can picture a funnel in your mind (or find a funnel in your kitchen drawer), you'll know that the top of a funnel is wide to catch all the liquid you're introducing to it. Similarly, with a marketing funnel, a large number of prospects will enter your funnel at the top and discover your brand for the first time. Not everyone will continue to show interest in your brand after entering the funnel, but a few will continue moving down the funnel as it becomes more narrow. In the middle of the funnel, the customers will learn more about your brand and evaluate your products. The funnel becomes even more narrow, and you will lose a few more potential customers. At the bottom of the funnel, the most qualified customers make their purchases.

Unlike a real funnel, which keeps all the liquid within it, a marketing funnel will only hold your most qualified prospects. Not everyone you target will ultimately be a good fit for your jewelry brand, and that's okay - you can't please everyone! The funnel has a funny way of weeding out the people who shouldn't be there anyway.

Search for "marketing funnel" on Google Images, and you'll find a few different visual interpretations, some with numerous steps and others with just a few. The terminology also varies from one model to another. For the sake of simplicity, I'll divide the funnel into three distinct parts: Awareness, Consideration, and Action. Consumers at each step of the funnel have different needs and respond to different types of marketing messages and tactics.

Awareness

If you're a new jewelry brand, or you're currently focused on expanding your reach to new markets, then you'll want to invest your time, energy, and effort into optimizing the top of your funnel: Awareness. Pouring prospects into the top of your funnel doesn't mean trying to capture everyone; filling your funnel should still be a focused effort, and your goal should be to reach as many of your target customers as possible. Some tactics for bolstering the top of your marketing funnel include a brand awareness Facebook campaign, presence at an event or trade show, search engine optimization, and enticing social media posts. At this stage, you'll want to pique your target customers' curiosity and tug at their heart strings, so you'll want to efficiently communicate something essential and with emotional resonance about your brand mission, vision, and values.

Consideration

In the middle of the funnel, prospects are already curious, and you've piqued their interest. They'll likely follow you on social media and even sign up for your email marketing newsletter, if you offer them a clear and strong call to action. Prospects in the Consideration step of your funnel will want to know more about your reputation, your products, and your values as a business. Some may even want to know, "Who else is wearing this jewelry?" and "Does this jewelry match my style and lifestyle?" Some tactics for strengthening the middle of your funnel include Facebook retargeting ads, email marketing campaigns, blogs posts, and direct engagement with these people on social media. At this stage, you'll want to build trust with the prospect through consistency, and you'll want to continue reminding her that your brand not only exists but that it's also relevant.

Action

At the bottom of the funnel, your prospects are most interested in details like product reviews, product descriptions, customer service information, shipping details, return policies, and more. They're the ones who are adding products to their carts and trying to decide whether or not to enter their payment information. They might be comparing your jewelry to similar products made by your competitors, and they're probably asking themselves questions like, "Do I really need this right now?" and "Can I afford this?". To optimize the bottom of your funnel, you can utilize product-specific Facebook retargeting ads, send automated abandoned cart emails, add social proof and user-generated content to your website and social media, and improve your product pages. At this stage, your soon-to-be customer wants to feel confident and certain.

Keep in mind that the time to get a prospect through the funnel can be very short (hours) or even very long (years) - or anywhere in between. Typically, fashion jewelry brands will have short funnels, since price points are low, and customers are risking very little by making a purchase. However, for most fine jewelry brands, the funnel can be very long, since most customers aren't ready to buy right away. If you have high price points, then you need to be prepared to nurture those prospects for the long haul.

One of the most important reasons you should get familiar with your funnel is that it can help you diagnose leaks. For example, if you have a high abandoned cart rate, or your ads simply aren't converting, then you're probably not helping your target customers transition effectively from Consideration to Action. Marketing funnels are extremely important when you're planning Facebook ad campaigns, since Facebook's ad objectives are based on the concept of a funnel; your goal in setting up multiple campaigns should be to lead customers through the funnel, specifically by casting your net and then retargeting prospects who have visited your site.

In addition, understanding a marketing funnel can help you set realistic expectations about your marketing efforts and also enable you to gain insight into your customers' path to purchase. Building brand awareness doesn't necessarily mean you'll be selling many products at first. However, it does give you the opportunity to create relationships with the people who discover your brand, so you can continue to market to them as they work their way down to the more narrow part of the funnel, where they become more likely to buy.

Single channel vs. multichannel vs. omni-channel

During the COVID-19 pandemic, many jewelry brands that only sold their products through one sales channel realized how important it is to diversify and to not put "all their eggs in one basket". Jewelry brands that were only available in brick-and-mortar stores scrambled to set up ecommerce shops. Even the brands with online stores rushed to optimize their ecommerce presence and reach customers in new ways - through virtual trunk shows, social commerce, and more.

So what's the difference between single channel, multichannel, and omnichannel? Which one is right for your jewelry brand, and how should you adjust your marketing efforts to match your sales strategy? With single-channel commerce, a jewelry brand is selling through one channel only. For example, that brand may have a brick-and-mortar store, an Etsy shop, or an ecommerce storefront. Marketing for a single-channel brand is pretty one-dimensional and straightforward, since your goal is to simply drive foot or digital traffic to your store. However, the single-channel model can also be limiting, since most consumers today are always moving between sales channels and often making purchasing decisions based on convenience and comparisons. Your preferred way of selling may not be your target customer's preferred way of buying. By not providing options, you may be alienating consumers.

With multichannel, a jewelry brand sells its products through a number of separate and independent channels. For example, the brand may sell on its own ecommerce website, in a proprietary brick-and-mortar boutique, in a retailer's boutique, on a retailer's ecommerce site, at trunk shows and pop-up shops, and more. For the most part, each channel acts as an independent silo.

With each channel, the jewelry brand may have different types of customers that respond better to different types of marketing. For example, the brand may make jewelry that appeals to many different generations; while the Millennials may prefer to shop the brand's ecommerce site, the Boomers may prefer to shop in store or at trunk shows. As a result, the jewelry brand must also segment its marketing efforts. Visitors to the website may respond best to Facebook retargeting ads, while shoppers at the trunk show may enjoy personalized email invitations to future events.

According to data published in the *Harvard Business Review*, 73% of all customers use multiple channels during their purchase journey and will only buy once they feel like they have enough information to make an informed decision.[62] To follow and track your customer journey seamlessly, you should strive to provide an omnichannel experience. Omnichannel is different from multichannel because the channels are not treated as separate silos. Instead, the jewelry brand expects that the customer will move seamlessly from one channel to another and then buy whenever she's ready to buy. As a result, all marketing must also be integrated and follow the customer along the journey and through the funnel.

One great example of a jewelry brand that's embracing omnichannel and marketing is Kendra Scott; they're constantly anticipating how consumers want to experience and buy their jewelry. Within days of closing all their stores in March 2020, in the thick of the COVID-19 pandemic, they were able to implement curbside pickup, buy-online-pick-up-in-store (BOPIS), and ship from store options for customers.[63] These changes now allow customers to shop conveniently and seamlessly.

In May 2020, Kendra Scott also introduced a virtual try-on tool, which allows customers to "try on" products without ever visiting a store.[64] Fewer customers may have been visiting retail stores, but they still wanted to have an in-store shopping experience in a safe way. With this virtual try-on tool, Kendra Scott gains data about the customer's preferred product selections, so when the customer is ready to buy, the ecommerce site can provide personalized product recommendations.

With omnichannel marketing, personalized marketing campaigns can follow a customer's behaviors. For example, if a customer abandons her cart, she may receive an email reminding her that she can also pick up the product at her local store instead of waiting for the product to be shipped. The experience is better integrated for your customer, and the resulting data is more useful for you. You can gain amazing insights about your customers and their path to purchase.

In 2020, omnichannel is definitely an ideal model, since more consumers expect to be able to purchase their desired item in whatever way is most convenient to them. Today's consumers are empowering themselves with information and shopping in an intelligent way, so they expect retailers to keep up with them - or get left behind.

However, not every jewelry brand has the resources to execute an omnichannel strategy immediately. For example, if you don't already have an ecommerce store, then you'll have to spend more time and money on building out the full digital experience for your brand. A brick-and-mortar-only store will want to start by embracing multichannel. They may even want to market their online presence differently to attract a new customer base. From there, a jewelry brand can focus on transitioning from multichannel to omnichannel incrementally. For example, a brand can start by experimenting with social commerce in addition to ecommerce. They can offer location-based recommendations that show the customer where she can try on the products.

Omnichannel also has the potential to improve relationships between jewelry brands and retailers. I've heard from many jewelry entrepreneurs that they struggle to get their products featured in retail stores. Furthermore, they're sick and tired of the consignment model and wish that retailers would buy their products outright. Retailers want to know that the products will sell before they decide to purchase inventory. However, if more direct-to-consumer jewelry brands followed an omnichannel model, they could focus on driving potential customers to all their channels - including their retail partners - with the goal of creating a seamless customer experience.

With this omnichannel model, retailers could serve as mini distribution sites, even if the products are only in store on consignment, and those retailers could fulfill orders for customers who live nearby. Over time, the jewelry brand could build trust with the retailers, and the popularity and profitability of the products could be established. It's a win-win situation: the jewelry brand gains more exposure by maintaining a presence on store shelves and at other physical locations, and the retailers win because the jewelry brands are treating them as an integrated channel, not as an "other".

Not only can an omnichannel approach help you stay top-of-mind with your target customers, but it can also offer convenience and flexibility, two things consumers have been trained to expect in an Amazon age. They'll be more inclined to buy from you when they're ready, since the product selection and purchasing process will embody everything that makes shopping "fun", as it should be, whether it's being done online or in person.

CHAPTER SEVENTEEN

ECOMMERCE BEST PRACTICES

Some of the top ecommerce platforms today include Magento, WooCommerce, and Shopify/Shopify Plus. Before I discuss the advantages and disadvantages of each one of these platforms, I want to first share the differences between open source and SaaS ecommerce platforms. Side note: there's also a category of ecommerce platforms called Commerce as a Service or CaaS, which gives you the option to add ecommerce functionality to an existing website. For the sake of simplicity, I'll only be focusing on the first two categories, which will offer the most robust ecommerce functionality for your jewelry brand.

With an open source ecommerce platform, you get full access to the code, and you'll need to find a way to host the site. Some businesses choose open source ecommerce platforms because they allow for full customization of design and layout, the potential for increased security, and the option to choose from a larger selection of third-party integrations. On the other hand, an SaaS ecommerce platform takes care of hosting and offers business owners a "plug and play" solution, so they don't have to worry as much about maintenance and security.

Popular open source ecommerce platforms

Magento Open Source – Launched in 2007, Magento is an open-source e-commerce platform written in the PHP programming language. This ecommerce solution "delivers the features you need to build and grow a unique online store from the ground up", according to the Magento website.[65] Well-known brands like Sergio Rossi and Christian Louboutin use Magento Open Source. Downloading and using the system costs nothing, but you'll need to hire a developer to help you setup and configure it and a designer to help you customize the user interface. Benefits include control and scalability, flexibility, and robust community support.

According to data from Magento itself, it handles more than $155 billion in transactions every year.[66] Please note that this number also include merchants using Magento's other solutions, like Magento Commerce Cloud.

WooCommerce – Built on the WordPress content management system, WooCommerce is an open-source ecommerce platform that's free to download and use. According to stats from Built With, more than 3.5 million live websites are currently using WooCommerce.[67]

One reason business owners choose WooCommerce is because they already have a robust content marketing strategy on WordPress, and they're seeking an ecommerce solution that can integrate seamlessly with their content. Another reason they prefer WooCommerce is because it's kept lean, so they can add just the features they want. To use WooCommerce, you'll also need to hire a developer to help you setup and configure it and a designer to help you customize the user interface.

Popular SaaS ecommerce platforms

Magento Commerce Cloud – In 2016, Magento launched Magento Commerce Cloud, which is hosted in the cloud on Amazon Web Services. Current Magento Commerce Cloud customers include Helly Hansen, Oliver Sweeney, Osprey London, and Soak & Sleep.

According to an article from Paul Rogers, "Licensing fees for Magento Commerce start at $23,000 per year, obviously on top of the website build / development costs (agency / developers). I would say that an average Magento Commerce build is likely to be anywhere from $150k – $1m."[68] As you can probably tell from the pricing, this solution is better suited for an enterprise rather than a small business.

Shopify/Shopify Plus – While Shopify is designed for small to medium sized businesses, the newer Shopify Plus is designed for large enterprise businesses and is a direct competitor to Magento Commerce Cloud. Shopify is a complete commerce platform that lets small business owners grow and manage their ecommerce businesses. With the platform, business owners are able to create and customize an online store, sell in multiple locations, and manage their inventory and payments.

Not only is Shopify affordable, with plans starting at just $29/month, but it's also very easy to setup and use, with a slim learning curve. Shopify offers a number of free customizable theme layouts. In addition, theme developers sell additional Shopify-approved themes in the Shopify Theme Store.

In contrast, Shopify Plus is an enterprise-level ecommerce solution on par with Magento Commerce Cloud, and it's ideal for brands bringing in $60,000/month or more in sales. As an ecommerce business grows, all aspects of managing it become more complex. Shopify Plus offers businesses a scalable solution.

According to data from Shopify, companies making $1M-500M are growing an average of 126% YoY on Shopify Plus.[69] More than 5,300 brands use Shopify Plus.[70]

I simply scratched the surface of ecommerce by discussing only a handful of ecommerce platforms. In reality, there are dozens of ecommerce platforms, and you'll need to assess your current business needs and future goals before you make a decision. As a side note, I do want to explain why I did not include platforms like Wix and Squarespace in this round-up of ecommerce platforms. These platforms were created to help people quickly build all-purposes websites, not necessarily ecommerce websites. They both now support ecommerce because they had to start offering ecommerce solutions in order to compete with Shopify. While it's true that you can build a very beautiful website with either Wix or Squarespace, you may not be able to build a website that's optimized for the ecommerce user experience that your customers expect today. You definitely won't be able to build an ecommerce website that will scale with you as your jewelry business grows.

In general, I would recommend Shopify to small business owners who want a plug-and-play ecommerce solution that can give them a taste of what it's like to sell online. Larger businesses will need to assess their budget, challenges, and goals before speaking to an ecommerce web developer and deciding which solution will best help them scale and serve their customers.

Social commerce

If you run an ecommerce jewelry store, and you're already taking advantage of social media marketing, then you're familiar with how your social media presence can help direct new customers to your ecommerce store. But have you ever heard the term "social commerce"? With social commerce, a brand creates a personalized and targeted shopping experience within a social media platform like Instagram, Facebook, or Pinterest, so the customer can shop without ever leaving the social media platform. In addition, social commerce can refer to a brand that has incorporated a social experience into its own app or website.

As you learned from Chapter 16, most consumers want to be able to shop where they are, so they don't want to abandon their social media browsing to purchase something they see in a post. Instead, they expect a seamless and frictionless buying experience. To meet consumer expectations, social media platforms like Instagram and Facebook have introduced new features to make that buying experience possible: buy buttons within social posts, "shoppable" posts and stories, social media ads that invite the customer to "buy now", and peer-to-peer buying and selling.

As a jewelry brand, you may already be leveraging social commerce without even realizing it. For example, if you're taking full advantage of Instagram Shopping, then you're tagging your products in your photos, videos, and stories and then turning those posts into opportunities for Instagram users to shop. Instagram is already taking social commerce to a whole new level by offering Instagram Checkout, which allows customers to purchase products within Instagram, without ever having to leave the app and going to the retailer's website.

Social commerce can eliminate steps in the conversion funnel, help you respond quickly to customer queries, and get your products shared. First, statistics show that customers are less likely to buy a product with each step they must take in the conversion funnel. For example, if your customer must interrupt social media browsing to visit your website and then add a product to a cart and ultimately enter payment information, the customer will be more prone to abandoning the purchase and leaving your store behind. When you can combine the shopping experience with the social experience, then you're streamlining the purchase journey. Second, customers who are shopping on a social media platform expect to also be able to interact with your jewelry brand in the same way they'd interact with friends on social media – through DMs and comments. They can ask you questions directly, and you have the chance to build personal relationships with them. Finally, on a social media platform, it's easy for customers to share and recommend your products to their friends. In addition, customers can easily save your products to purchase later, if they're not ready to click "buy" in that moment.

For social commerce to work effectively, your ecommerce site must absolutely be optimized for mobile shopping, since most people engage in social media activity on their smartphones. In addition, you must be committed to investing money and time into your photography, which will represent your brand on social media. Finally, you'll want to prioritize building trust with customers and focusing on creating lasting relationships with them.

Have you heard the recent announcement from Instagram about the platform's new feature called Instagram Checkout? Different from Shopping on Instagram – which allows businesses to add product tags that provide more information and a link to purchase – Checkout allows users to make a purchase without leaving the Instagram app.

Homepage

One of the biggest mistakes that ecommerce jewelry entrepreneurs make is failing to consider the similarities between ecommerce and brick-and-mortar jewelry stores and then forgetting to implement important merchandising and technical best practices in their digital storefront. Even though a brick-and-mortar store requires physical space, while an ecommerce store does not, the two types of stores actually share a lot in common. Ecommerce entrepreneurs can actually learn a lot from brick-and-mortar store owners.

The CEO of a New York City-based digital agency once told me something about storefronts I'll never forget. To paraphrase him, many jewelry brands with a brick-and-mortar presence invest significant amounts of money into prime real estate for their stores. Their goal is to gain coveted foot traffic and the brand awareness that comes with having a beautiful jewelry store and signage associated with their name. Think about Tiffany & Co.'s flagship store on Fifth Avenue in Manhattan or David Yurman and Harry Winston's stores on Rodeo Drive in Beverly Hills. How much would it cost you to set up a brick-and-mortar jewelry store in a prime location where you live?

Unfortunately, many jewelry entrepreneurs view ecommerce as the cheap alternative to a brick-and-mortar jewelry store. Yes, it's true that setting up a Shopify storefront probably won't cost you as much as a Rodeo Drive address. However, the attitude that ecommerce is a budget sales channel is dangerous and damaging. With ecommerce, you may not be making a serious investment in real estate, but you should be making a serious investment in website development, ecommerce optimization, and marketing. If not, how can you expect your target customers to pay attention and take you seriously?

If you owned a brick-and-mortar jewelry store, you would likely do everything in your power to keep that store looking clean, fresh, and interesting. Let's say you have a store window in a busy part of town, and the passersby are always looking in your window. If you never update the window, then the regulars probably won't bother to look. In addition, if your window display isn't immaculate and clean, then you'll send the wrong message about your store. Your ecommerce homepage functions a lot like that store window.

What are the best practices for homepages, and which features and elements should your homepage definitely include? As you think about the following features and elements, remember: the goal is to actually get your customers off your homepage, so they can shop products within your site.

Navigation

The navigation of your ecommerce website is one of the most important aspects of your homepage, since most customers will want to quickly leave your homepage to either view your products or learn more about you. If your homepage is even the least bit complicated, then customers won't have the patience to figure out how to navigate your site, and they'll go to your competitors instead.

When building your website navigation, you should not be creative or fancy. Instead, you'll want to emulate the navigation structure of other popular and successful ecommerce websites and follow their standardized formats, since your users will already be used to using them. For example, most ecommerce stores feature their navigation menu horizontally across the top of the page, and the navigation should move with the user while he or she scrolls.

The most difficult part about structuring a main navigation menu is keeping the main menu short and concise, including only the most important pages. As much as possible, minimize your use of dropdown menus. At the same time, you're probably better off having a dropdown menu than showcasing all your jewelry categories across the top of the page. In addition to featuring an intuitive and streamlined navigation bar, you'll also want to include a website search box, so customers can always search if they can't immediately find what they need from your navigation.

A visual story

If you have professionally-shot images of models wearing your jewelry, then your homepage is the ideal place to display them in such a way that helps you tell your brand story. The large banner image that stretches across your homepage "above the fold" (the part of your site that's visible before you scroll) is known as the "hero" image.

As I mentioned earlier, your homepage is your shop window, which you should change and update regularly. The designated space for your hero image gives you the opportunity to showcase seasonal items, new products/collections, or even limited-time promotions. Commit to updating it regularly. Alongside your images, use strong calls to action and copywriting that support your brand voice, your unique value proposition, and the lifestyle you represent. The visual story should unfold as the user scrolls further down the page.

Make it easy for the customer to shop

Where should your customer begin his or her journey, and how can you make the experience easy and seamless? Of course, if your customer is completely new to your brand and your products, then that person wouldn't know where to begin. For this exercise, consider the in-store experience. An effective salesperson in a jewelry boutique might approach a new customer and say, "Welcome! Is this your first time shopping with us?" Followup questions may include, "What can I help you find today?" or "Would you like me to recommend some pieces?"

Similarly, you'll want to consider how you can mimic this same in-store experience for your ecommerce customers. Would you like your customers to view your new products or bestsellers? If so, feature them clearly on the homepage. Would you like your customers to know about your sale items? If so, call them out on the homepage.

Ecommerce platforms are becoming more and more sophisticated, and jewelry brands are able to offer their customers personalized experiences, based on the source that brought them to the site, their location (derived from an IP address), and even their shopping history. If you're not making your customers feel welcome, then you're missing out on opportunities for growth and loyalty.

Compelling calls to action and "shop" buttons

Are you inviting your customers to explore your site? Now that you've welcomed them to your "home", you'll want to take them on the journey of your brand. Where would you like your customers to go, and what would you like them to experience?

If you ever read "choose your own adventure" books as a child, you may remember that, at the end of each chapter, you could choose from two different options. The reader could continue to one page to experience one adventure or to another to experience a different adventure. The curious and motivated readers would continue turning the pages because they were invested in the story. Similarly, aim to engage your customers deeply in the experience.

Build trust

Shoppers who are new to your brand and website will likely be scanning for trust signals like product reviews, customer service information, and trust badges (certificates confirming that your website is secure). Make sure that your customer service information is clearly displayed on your homepage and that it's extremely easy for a user to contact customer service. You may even want to consider adding live chat functionality to your homepage, so a customer can always feel confident and supported while browsing your site. Success indicators like awards and other forms of recognition are also great elements to add to your homepage.

Shipping and promotions

If you offer free shipping, then you'll definitely want to display this information front and center, since your shipping terms can make or break a shopper's willingness to buy. In addition, you'll want to display any promotions or specials you may be having at any given time.

Make sure your homepage is responsive

When a site is "responsive", it means that it's just as easy to navigate on a desktop computer as it is to use on a mobile device like a smartphone or tablet. To make your homepage responsive, you'll want to optimize your images for speedy loading and make sure the navigation translates to a small screen. Ensure that your typography is easy to read on a mobile device and that anything clickable is optimized for touchscreens, not only for cursors. A web developer can help you check for these things.

Keep it simple

If you have a small product assortment, then curating your homepage will likely be easier than if you have a very large product assortment. Too many products can make your homepage feel unapproachable and even overwhelming.

Have you ever stood in a grocery store or drugstore and felt completely overwhelmed by the selection of products for any given category? For example, when you need to buy a new toothbrush, you may see about 30 different toothbrush options on the display rack. If you're not loyal to any one brand, you may have no idea which one to buy. You scan quickly for any promotions or special features, or you might even look for your favorite color. If you're in a rush, you'll probably just settle for the first one that catches your eye.

A toothbrush is a low-priced purchase, so customers don't risk very much when faced with the overwhelming decision of committing to one. However, jewelry can potentially be a very high-priced purchase, so the feeling of overwhelm will definitely turn off a customer who's on the fence about buying. Keep your homepage simple and set the expectation that shopping your site will be fun and enjoyable, not a stressful burden.

A/B testing

How do you know that your homepage is effective and actually helping you make sales? Instead of committing to one homepage layout, you may want to test two versions using A/B testing (for more information about A/B testing, refer back to Chapter 3). You may have an idea about what your customers want, but you won't actually know what they want until you see how they behave while shopping your site. A/B testing can provide you with insights about your overall layout, your choice of hero images, your email marketing pop-ups, your navigation, and more. A web developer can help you implement and then analyze a strategic A/B test.

Your homepage is your storefront; it can help establish trust and credibility, and it can sometimes make the first impression with your customers. However, some of your customers may actually be finding your site through your product pages and not your homepage.

If you consider how consumers seek products using search engines, most shoppers are probably searching for a specific piece of jewelry and then comparing the results from the various brands offering that product. They're not searching for your

JEWELRY MARKETING JOY · 259

brand name unless they know you and want to shop from you specifically. As a result, your product page - not your homepage - will likely be the search engine result, since the product page is ideally optimized for a specific search term like "18K gold diamond tennis bracelet".

In addition, when you're tagging products on Instagram, that tag will take your customers to a product page and not your homepage (though that will rapidly change as more consumers expect to shop within social media apps themselves). Even though your homepage may not always be the first customer touchpoint, it's still important, since your customer will refer to it for trust signals, product recommendations, promotions, customer service information, and more.

Product pages

If you're not spending more time, energy, effort, and money on your jewelry product pages than you are on basically every other part of your ecommerce website, you could be sabotaging your conversion rate. Yes, product pages are more important than even your homepage!

Above all, product pages are important because of how your customers search for your products on Google. Unless your customers are seeking a specific brand, they're not typing a brand name into the Google search box. Instead, they're looking for a product type or product category. For example, if they're hunting for an emerald-cut engagement ring, they're not necessarily starting their search with "James Allen" or "Blue Nile". Instead, they want to see all the options available and to comparison shop. They'll search for "emerald-cut engagement ring", and Google will yield product and product category pages, but not homepages. Customers finding you through Google are rarely landing on your homepage first.

The fact that your product pages are helping your ideal customers find you presents you with many opportunities, since product pages can easily be optimized with keywords. You can only include so much SEO-friendly content on your homepage, but you can add many keywords on your product pages, especially in product descriptions, image alt tags, page titles, headings, meta descriptions, and more.

Once you get your ideal customer to your site, you want to keep that person there for as long as possible, and you want to encourage that person to browse other products too. An engaging, well-designed product page that's optimized for mobile browsing will keep your target customer on the page, long enough for her to at least add a product to her cart and ideally to make a purchase. However, if she's not ready to purchase now, she should at least feel inspired to share the page, sign up for your email newsletter, save or "favorite" the product, or bookmark the product page for later, so she can do further research. Hint: you can see how long users are staying on your product pages by viewing stats like Bounce Rate and average session duration in Google Analytics.

Finally, product pages matter tremendously if you're going to invest money in paid advertising, especially ads that showcase specific products and drive your target customers to your product pages. Most of the target customers you'll be reaching with your ads will only be mildly familiar with your brand, so their click will be a sign of passing curiosity. They're not necessarily motivated to buy your product at that time, and they'll be quick to abandon your product page if it doesn't immediately interest them. As a result, you must catch their attention and impress them quickly.

Now that you know why you absolutely must optimize your product pages if you hope to sell your jewelry on your ecommerce store, you're probably wondering how you can get started and start boosting your conversion rate. Keep reading for some essential product page optimization tips.

Focus on getting reviews and social proof

Consider how you've made online purchases in the past. Given the choice between two versions of the same product, both at the same price points and with the same specifications, wouldn't you choose the retailer who had more positive reviews? When you're searching for products on Amazon, you may even sort by top-rated products, so you can weed out the poorly-rated options. If your customers don't see reviews on your product pages, then they'll be very hesitant to trust you. Customer testimonials and user-submitted photos and videos are also excellent forms of social proof.

Consider color psychology

You may be surprised to discover that color matters tremendously in ecommerce. Some colors will encourage shoppers to buy more readily, while other colors will turn people away. According to a research paper titled "Impact of color on marketing", "...colors can contribute not only to differentiating products from competitors, but also to influencing moods and feelings – positively or negatively – and therefore, to attitude towards certain products".[71] However, it's nearly impossible to make generalizations about color, like red is bad, and green is good. Instead, you'll want to consider factors like your target audience and the emotions you'd like to convey.

Use high-quality product images and videos

In my opinion, the one quality that sets an amateurish ecommerce website apart from a professional one is consistency in product photography. Product photos should follow a specific standard, which should be implemented throughout the site, across all products. Your primary product images should be well-lit and shot against a white background. They should all be the same size, showing the scale of each jewelry product. Secondary product images can show different perspectives and tell a story. Product videos and 360-degree views allow the customer to experience the product in a more realistic way. Finally, your images must load quickly and be optimized to scale for mobile devices.

Communicate your brand and unique value proposition

If someone finds your product page on Google, they likely know nothing about your brand. Just because the product page is focused on your product doesn't mean you can't also communicate your brand story and unique value proposition. Write the product description in the tone that matches your brand, choose a unique product title that's representative of your brand personality, showcase additional product photos that really capture the essence of what makes you unique. Your brand colors, logo, and other distinguishing features should all be visible. In addition, if the customer does want to learn more about your business, she should be able to easily navigate to the homepage, an "About" page, or a customer service page.

Make it easy to get help

Speaking of customer service, you want to show your customer that it's easy for her to get assistance if she needs it. A customer will be very hesitant to buy from a lesser-known brand if she feels like she can't easily contact them. To build trust, try implementing a customer service chat feature on your product pages. Or, include some of your basic customer service policies – like free returns, money-back guarantee, or complimentary repairs – somewhere near your product description. The more she feels comfortable shopping from you, the more likely she'll be to make the purchase.

What have you done lately to optimize your product pages? To set a baseline for yourself, check out your Google Analytics data and make note of your Bounce Rate and average time spent on page. After that, try making some changes and updates to your product pages to see if those metrics improve. Furthermore, you can try testing and experiment with two different versions of your product pages to see which one performs better than the other.

Product descriptions

With my background in creative writing, I personally love writing product descriptions. I find them to be extremely challenging in the best way, not only because the short word count is limiting but also because finding new things to say about jewelry can be difficult ("beautiful" gets old quickly). To find out how to improve your product descriptions, which will enhance the customer experience and help you tell the story of your products, follow these tips.

Keep target customers in mind

If I haven't already driven home the point that you need to consider your target customers at all times, then here's one more reminder: you need to know and imagine your target customers when you're writing product descriptions for them. Is she an educated, creative professional who enjoys reading literary fiction in her spare time? If so, you may want to write poetic product descriptions. Is she a Gen-Zer whose primary method of communication is text messaging? If so, you may want to write short and conversational product descriptions. You need to understand the types of messaging your target customer is used to receiving - and then emulate those formats.

Embody your brand voice

If your brand were a person, how would he or she describe your products? If you've done all the work that I described in Chapter 5, then you should be intimately familiar with your brand identity, and you should understand how your brand communicates with its customers. Is the tone excited and hurried, or is it elegant?

For a great example, check out the ecommerce website for Cornelia Webb, a jewelry brand inspired by the landscape of bodies. The designer is committed to environmental consciousness, and she considers how her designs affect the wearer's physical and emotional well-being. I think her product descriptions, like this one for her "Warped Multi-Stone Ring", capture her brand voice perfectly: "A ring to fall in love with over and over. It's a very special piece with the contrasting shapes of semi-precious gemstones, the style speaks of past times for a bright mission, the one we all have going forward."[72] She then describes the healing properties of each gemstone included in the ring. Don't be afraid to get specific with your voice.

Consider search engine optimization

No one knows for sure how much including SEO keywords in product descriptions impacts a website's search engine ranking, but it certainly can't hurt to optimize your descriptions for Google. According to Shopify's Help Center, you should be adding SEO keywords to page titles, meta descriptions, ALT tags, and page content (basically product descriptions).[73] Before you can add keywords to your product descriptions, you first need to decide which ones you'd like to target. For more information, you can refer back to Chapter 8.

Tell a story when possible

While your product photos can be worth a thousand words, as the saying goes, they can't express everything. According to research from DeBeers, consumers have been making more meaningful jewelry purchases during the COVID-19 lockdown. In fact, "56 percent of respondents felt gifts should be meaningful, over and above being practical, functional or fun".[74] If you're looking for ways to show your customers how your jewelry can be meaningful, then you'll definitely want to focus on refining your product descriptions.

When possible, tell a story about your product. For example, thanks to the product details for the Double X Crossover Ring on the David Yurman site,[75] I learned that the designer's X Collection was inspired by Sybil Yurman's painting of the ancient mark. On the Tiffany & Co. website, I discovered that the pieces from the brand's Paper Flowers collection are inspired by the idea of abstract flower petals, which represent femininity and industrial modernity.[76] What is the inspiration behind the piece? What special meaning or value do the materials possess? What was involved in making the piece? You can answer these questions in your description.

268 · LARYSSA WIRSTIUK

Make your descriptions easy to scan

With your product descriptions, you'll want to strike a balance between richness and scannability. According to research about how users read websites, 79 percent of people always scanned any new page they came across; only 16 percent read word-by-word.[77] While you can't just assume that no one will read your product descriptions, you also can't assume they will read your product descriptions from beginning to end. To improve your scannability, you'll want to be concise and specific, incorporate bullet points, use straightforward and objective language, and consider how the text looks on the page. If you're able to incorporate more white space by increasing the distance between lines or improving the contrast between the page color and font color, you'll be more likely to keep users engaged and reading.

Use specific adjectives but don't rely too heavily on them

In the previous section, I mentioned that you'll want to use straightforward and objective language in order to improve scannability. Of course, it can be difficult to tell a compelling story or adjust your tone when you're not using elaborate language. I'm not suggesting you drop all your adjectives or "feeling" words altogether. Instead, be very intentional and specific about the words you do choose.

For example, instead of using generic adjectives like "beautiful" and "luxurious", you can try some specific adjectives that pack a greater punch - and then use less of them. A resource like Thesaurus.com will be integral in helping you find alternatives like "enchanting", "refined", or "opulent". The right words for your product will depend on your target customer and your individual brand voice.

Writing product descriptions is more difficult than most jewelry entrepreneurs realize. After writing just a few, you may start to wonder, "How many different ways can I describe one of our rings?" Hiring a professional copywriter can take your product descriptions from generic to compelling. They may not be the factor that turns a browser into a life-long customer, but they will communicate your brand's mission and values, build trust with your target customers, and provide whatever information a photo cannot supply.

According to a June 2020 report about the future of ecommerce from Emarketer, US ecommerce sales growth was expected to surge to 18.0%, the highest on record since they started calculating the metric in 2008.[78] The popularity of ecommerce is only becoming more pervasive, and your jewelry brand must provide an exceptional digital customer experience in order to attract new customers and retain existing ones. Otherwise, they'll quickly lose interest and visit your competitors - just a few clicks away.

CHAPTER EIGHTEEN

MANAGING GROWTH

As your business grows, you'll need to scale your marketing to accommodate growth. To do that, you'll need to consistently revisit your marketing strategy, plan, and consider your marketing budget. You definitely don't want to scale your marketing unless you've taken the time and effort to measure the effectiveness of your past marketing campaigns. Of course, why would you move forward with something and continue doing it if you're not quite sure that it works? Once the data helps you feel fairly confident that your marketing efforts are producing your desired results, then you'll want to take them to the next level by investing more money into them and/or expanding your reach.

Scaling up may also mean scaling back a little. Just because your business is experiencing growth doesn't mean you can spend indiscriminately. Instead, you'll want to take this time to assess your progress. What have you done in the past that you

272 · LARYSSA WIRSTIUK

can leave behind? For example, you may have invested in certain tools to support your marketing and business development efforts. However, those same tools may no longer be relevant or useful; you can drop them or replace them with tools that are better suited to your needs.

You'll also want to make sure your team is ready to handle the growth that will come with scaling your marketing. Do you know who will be handling the new marketing initiatives? Do you have a system in place to handle order fulfillment? Do you have an ecommerce expert who can help you when your website gets overloaded with orders? Is your supply chain prepared? Scaling your marketing extends far beyond just scaling your marketing.

Automation will become even more important

We're not suggesting that your business should lose the human touch as you scale and grow. However, automation can complement your in-person interactions and ensure that you're maintaining relationships with customers and keeping in regular touch with them. Automation is especially important with email marketing, since you won't be able to track all your customer behavior on your own at any given time. Automated emails can follow up abandoned carts, give your customers product recommendations, congratulate customers on their purchases, and send customers discounts and other promotions based on their behaviors.

Remember to embrace personalization

As your business grows, your interactions with customers may start to seem slightly more impersonal, since you won't be able to communicate with them as often as you like. However, you can still incorporate personalization into your emails, your website experience, your ads, and more.

Measurement will become essential

In the past, you may have been able to make decisions based on your own observations of customer behavior and data. However, moving forward, you'll have too much activity to simply make intuitive decisions about your business. You need to continue setting those SMART goals, monitoring your progress, and then pivoting and adjusting your approach based on the numbers, not on a guess. A/B testing will also help you better understand what is and isn't resonating with your target audience.

To save yourself time, do your best to implement processes and make things repeatable

For example, do you reinvent the wheel every time you post on social media? Create a few graphic templates that you can follow. Instead of designing every email from scratch, you can recycle a few different looks. Not only will implementing processes save you time and leave less room for error, but it will also help you ensure that your brand remains consistent across all customer touchpoints.

Get the most mileage from all your marketing efforts

Did you recently publish a new blog post? Get the most from it by repurposing it in many ways; consider reinterpreting it as a video that you can publish to your YouTube channel or use elements of it for a social media post or email.

When should you hire a consultant?

While some of my clients knew intuitively that working with a jewelry marketing consultant was the right next step for their jewelry brand, others aren't so sure, and they ask, "Should we be investing in our marketing efforts now?"

I work with jewelry brands at every stage of business growth, so knowing when to invest in a jewelry marketing consultant doesn't necessarily have anything to do with how long a brand has been in business or how much profit's being made. Instead, it has everything to do with the jewelry brand's goals and their level of commitment to reach those goals. You may be ready to work with a jewelry marketing consultant if:

You don't have time to invest in marketing

When you first launched your jewelry brand, you may have performed every role in your business, from order fulfilment and customer service to marketing. However, now that your business is growing, you have less time to focus on anything that's not your primary strength or interest. If marketing isn't your forte, you'll want to find a marketing specialist who can join you on your journey as you grow your business.

You've reached a plateau

The marketing strategies that worked for you in the past simply aren't working anymore. You're so used to doing things the way they've been done that you're not sure how to pivot. A skilled marketing consultant can suggest new strategies that can help you get over your plateau and put you back on the fast track for growth.

You're thinking about rebranding or targeting a new audience

Will you be releasing new designs soon? Is it time for a brand refresh? Either way, you'll likely be targeting new customers. Whenever you're entering a new market, you'll want to seek the advice of a skilled marketing consultant, who can explain what you'll need to do to reach the right customers for your brand.

You never created a formal marketing strategy

Intoxicated by the excitement of starting a new jewelry business, you may have never made a formal marketing strategy. Now that you're growing, you feel overwhelmed by anything that has to do with marketing, and you need someone who can help you create and implement a plan. A strategy can establish appropriate expectations and outline the steps you'll need to take to reach your goals.

You can't stay focused

Many jewelry businesses struggle with marketing because they gain momentum with a marketing strategy and then get distracted by something else related to their business. As a result, progress gets interrupted and delayed. A skilled marketing consultant can keep you on track and manage your marketing projects, so you stay accountable and continue moving forward.

You need a fresh perspective

Sometimes, as the owner of a jewelry business, you can't see the forest for the trees. When you're bogged down by everyday responsibilities, you lose perspective of your business and can't imagine new ways to think about and communicate your brand. The outside perspective of a marketing consultant can breathe innovation and positive change into your business.

You want to invest your marketing budget efficiently

When it comes to marketing today, you have so many options for spending your money. Should you set aside a budget for a Facebook ad campaign or Google pay per click campaign? Should you invest your money in optimizing your website for search engines, or should you hire a designer to redo your logo? Should you pay for event marketing? A skilled marketing consultant can advise you how to allocate your marketing budget effectively.

Marketing is joyful

At the end of the day, marketing is about creating and building relationships, and you should approach it the same way you would any important connection, like one you might have with a best friend, parent, sibling, or romantic partner. These bonds are built on pillars of trust, respect, support, and clear communication - all things that an effective brand should be providing its customers.

I'm passionate about marketing because it's a joyful and fulfilling process of matchmaking - connecting the consumers who dream with the brands that can make those dreams come true. Now I ask you this: whose dreams would you like to fulfill today, tomorrow, and beyond?

RECOMMENDED RESOURCES

Books

Purple Cow: Transform Your Business by Being Remarkable by Seth Godin

This Is Marketing: You Can't Be Seen Until You Learn to See by Seth Godin

Start with Why: How Great Leaders Inspire Everyone to Take Action by Simon Sinek

Get Scrappy: Smarter Digital Marketing for Businesses Big and Small by Nick Westergaard

Digital Publications

The Business of Fashion - https://www.businessoffashion.com/

INSTORE Magazine - https://instoremag.com/

Jewelry Ecomm - https://jewelryecomm.com/

JCK - https://www.jckonline.com/

Joy Joya Blog - https://joyjoya.com/blog/

Marketing Dive - https://www.marketingdive.com/

National Jeweler -
https://www.nationaljeweler.com/

Retail Dive - https://www.retaildive.com/

Social Media Today -
https://www.socialmediatoday.com/

WWD - https://wwd.com/

Podcasts

Joy Joya Jewelry Marketing Podcast

The Glossy Podcast

Laryssa Wirstiuk is the founder and creative director of Joy Joya, a digital marketing agency for jewelry brands. She's passionate about empowering and inspiring jewelry entrepreneurs and innovators. She's also the host of the Joy Joya Jewelry Marketing Podcast. For more information, visit **joyjoya.com**.

NOTES

[1] "Jewelry Market Size Worth $480.5 Billion By 2025: CAGR: 8.1%." Grand View Research, June 2019. https://www.grandviewresearch.com/press-release/global-jewelry-market.

[2] Dauriz, Linda, Nathalie Remy, and Thomas Tochtermann. "A Multifaceted Future: The Jewelry Industry in 2020." McKinsey & Company, February 1, 2014. https://www.mckinsey.com/industries/retail/our-insights/a-multifaceted-future-the-jewelry-industry-in-2020.

[3] "Tiffany Soleste® Emerald-Cut Halo Engagement Ring with a Diamond Platinum Band.: Tiffany & Co." Tiffany Soleste® emerald-cut halo engagement ring with a diamond platinum band. | Tiffany & Co. Accessed September 4, 2020. https://www.tiffany.com/engagement/engagement-rings/tiffany-soleste-emerald-cut-halo-engagement-ring-with-a-diamond-platinum-band-GRP10868/.

[4] Bates, Rob. "Signet Drops 'He Went to Jared' Tagline." JCK, November 8, 2018. https://www.jckonline.com/editorial-article/signet-drops-he-went-to-jared/.

[5] "2019 Edelman Trust Barometer Special Report." Edelman, June 2019. https://www.edelman.com/sites/g/files/aatuss191/files/2019-06/2019_edelman_trust_barometer_special_report_in_brands_we_trust.pdf.

[6] Jantsch, John. "How Long Should It Take For My Marketing To Work?" Duct Tape Marketing, February 12, 2007. https://ducttapemarketing.com/how-long-should-it-take-for-my-marketing-to-work/.

[7] "Data-Driven Marketing Strategy Survey Summary Report ." Ascend2, July 2017. http://ascend2.com/wp-content/uploads/2017/07/Ascend2-Data-Driven-Marketing-Strategy-Report-170714.pdf.

[8] Krebs, Brian. "Jared, Kay Jewelers Parent Fixes Data Leak." Krebs on Security, December 3, 2018. https://krebsonsecurity.com/2018/12/jared-kay-jewelers-parent-fixes-data-leak/.

[9] Nixon, George. "Meghan Markle's Favourite Jewellery Brand Missoma Hit by Cyber-Attack." This Is Money, December 17, 2019. https://www.thisismoney.co.uk/money/beatthescammers/article-7800919/Meghan-Markles-favourite-jewellery-brand-Missoma-hit-cyber-attack.html.

[10] Stidham, Kristina. "Claire's Suffers Data Breach, Payment Data Exposed." Total Retail, June 16, 2020. https://www.mytotalretail.com/article/claires-experiences-data-breach-potentially-exposing-online-payment-information/.

[11] Auxier, Brooke, Lee Rainie, Monica Anderson, Andrew Perrin, Madhu Kumar, and Erica Turner. "Americans and Privacy: Concerned, Confused and Feeling Lack of Control Over Their Personal Information." Pew Research Center, November 15, 2019. https://www.pewresearch.org/internet/2019/11/15/americans-and-privacy-concerned-confused-and-feeling-lack-of-control-over-their-personal-information/.

[12] Guttmann, A. "Topic: Personalized Marketing." Statista, January 4, 2019. https://www.statista.com/topics/4481/personalized-marketing/.

[13] "UK Regulators' Data Violations Fines Top $126.5M." PYMNTS.com, January 20, 2020. https://www.pymnts.com/news/security-and-risk/2020/uk-regulators-data-violations-fines-top-126-5m/.

[14] "How The GLD Shop Increased Conversions by 300% with A/B Tests." Justuno, August 30, 2017. https://www.justuno.com/blog/a-b-test-how-shopify-plus-merchant-the-gld-shop-increased-conversions-by-300/.

[15] Sullivan, Craig. "Hypothesis Kit 3." Medium, August 18, 2015. https://medium.com/@optimiseordie/hypothesis-kit-2-eff0446e09fc.

[16] Godin, Seth. Purple Cow: Transform Your Business by Being Remarkable. New York, NY: Portfolio, 2009.

[17] "About." Everlane. Accessed September 4, 2020. https://www.everlane.com/about.

[18] "The State of Brand Consistency." Lucidpress. Accessed September 5, 2020. https://www.lucidpress.com/pages/resources/report/the-impact-of-brand-consistency.

[19] Bates, Rob. "After a Down Year, Pandora Wants to Bring Back 'Passion.'" JCK, February 5, 2019. https://www.jckonline.com/editorial-article/pandora-bring-back-passion/.

[20] Keller, Kevin Lane. "Conceptualizing, Measuring, and Managing Customer-Based Brand Equity." Journal of Marketing 57, no. 1 (1993): 1–22. https://doi.org/10.2307/1252054.

[21] "State of Create: 2016." Adobe, 2016. https://www.adobe.com/content/dam/acom/en/max/pdfs/AdobeStateof Create_2016_Report_Final.pdf.

[22] Whelan, John. "Op-Ed: The Revolution Will Not Be Serifised: Why Every Luxury Brand's Logo Looks the Same." The Business of Fashion, January 25, 2019. https://www.businessoffashion.com/articles/opinion/the-revolution-will-not-be-serifised-why-every-luxury-brands-logo-looks-the-same-burberry-balmain-balenciaga.

[23] LaBarre, Suzanne. "The Hottest Branding Trend of the Year Is Also the Worst." Fast Company, December 11, 2018. https://www.fastcompany.com/90276496/the-hottest-branding-trend-of-the-year-is-also-the-worst.

[24] Di, Wei, Neel Sundaresan, Robinson Piramuthu, and Anurag Bhardwaj. "Is a Picture Really Worth a Thousand Words?: - on the Role of Images in e-Commerce." WSDM '14: Proceedings of the 7th ACM international conference on Web search and data mining, February 2014. https://dl.acm.org/doi/10.1145/2556195.2556226.

[25] "Content Marketing Infographic." Demand Metric. Accessed September 6, 2020. https://www.demandmetric.com/content/content-marketing-infographic.

[26] Patel, Neil. "When Can You Expect Your Content Marketing Efforts to Bear Fruit?" Neil Patel. Accessed September 6, 2020. https://neilpatel.com/blog/when-can-you-expect-your-content-marketing-efforts-to-bear-fruit/.

[27] Irvine, Mark. "Google Shopping Ads Benchmarks: Average CPC, CTR, Monthly Budget, & More." WordStream, May 1, 2020. https://www.wordstream.com/blog/ws/2019/04/01/shopping-ads-benchmarks.

[28] Tran, Tony. "Instagram Demographics That Matter to Social Media Marketers in 2020." Hootsuite, February 4, 2020. https://blog.hootsuite.com/instagram-demographics/.

[29] "Get Started on Instagram for Businesses." Instagram for Business. Accessed September 8, 2020. https://business.instagram.com/getting-started?ref=igb_carousel.

[30] "How to Plan for Holidays on Instagram." Instagram for Business, October 10, 2019. https://business.instagram.com/blog/how-to-plan-for-holidays-on-instagram/.

[31] Ibid.

[32] Aslam, Salman. "Facebook by the Numbers: Stats, Demographics & Fun Facts." Omnicore, April 4, 2020. https://www.omnicoreagency.com/facebook-statistics/.

[33] Chen, Jenn. "Social Media Demographics to Inform Your Brand's Strategy in 2020." Sprout Social. Accessed September 8, 2020. https://sproutsocial.com/insights/new-social-media-demographics/.

[34] Cialdini, Robert B. Influence: How and Why People Agree to Things. Quill, 1985.

[35] Godin, Seth. Tribes: We Need You to Lead Us. New York, NY: Portfolio, 2008.

[36] Packham, Alex. "What Is a Good Social Media Engagement Rate?" ContentCal, May 15, 2020. https://www.contentcal.io/blog/what-is-a-good-social-media-engagement-rate/.

[37] Branstrator, Brecken. "How Simon G. Used Local Influencers to Support Its Retailers." National Jeweler, July 17, 2019. https://www.nationaljeweler.com/majors/ecommerce/7901-how-simon-g-used-local-influencers-to-support-its-retailers.

[38] Ibid.

[39] Ibid.

[40] Eadie, Blair. "HOLIDAY STACKING // DAVID YURMAN: Atlantic-Pacific." Atlantic-Pacific, December 4, 2017. https://www.the-atlantic-pacific.com/2017/12/04/holiday-stacking-david-yurman/.

[41] "Case Study: Luxury Brand Marketing And An Unlikely Instagram Hero." Mediakix. Accessed September 8, 2020. https://mediakix.com/blog/luxury-brand-marketing-case-study-tiffany-and-co/.

[42] MISSOMA (@missomalondon). 2019. "Get ready for the ultimate jewellery mixtape." Instagram, August 13, 2019. https://www.instagram.com/p/B1GIJfZBwCB/.

[43] Naragon, Kristin. "Consumers Are Still Email Obsessed, But They're Finding More Balance." Adobe Blog, August 29, 2017. https://blog.adobe.com/en/2017/08/29/consumers-are-still-email-obsessed-but-theyre-finding-more-balance.html.

[44] "New Rules of Email Marketing [2019]." Campaign Monitor. Accessed September 12, 2020. https://www.campaignmonitor.com/resources/guides/email-marketing-new-rules/.

[45] Abramovich, Giselle. "15 Mind-Blowing Stats About Generation Z." CMO by Adobe, June 2019. https://cmo.adobe.com/articles/2019/6/15-mind-blowing-stats-about-generation-z.html.

[46] "The Freeman Data Benchmark Report for Corporate Marketers." Freeman. Accessed September 13, 2020. https://www.freeman.com/resources/data-report.

[47] "5 Stellar Examples of Successful Jewelry Digital Campaigns." Launchmetrics, August 2, 2018. https://www.launchmetrics.com/resources/blog/successful-jewelry-digital-campaigns.

[48] Elliott, Amy. "Metal & Smith Announces Plan for a Virtual Jewelry Trade Show This May." JCK, March 23, 2020. https://www.jckonline.com/editorial-article/metal-and-smith-virtual-trade-show/.

[49] Ibid.

[50] Elliott, Amy. "Tired of Trunk Shows? Try a 'Jewelry Styling' Event." JCK, October 30, 2018. https://www.jckonline.com/editorial-article/jewelry-styling-event/.

[51] Sawyer, Katie. "Event Budgeting: How To Master Your Event Budget." Eventbrite US Blog, February 7, 2019. https://www.eventbrite.com/blog/event-budget-guide-ds00/.

[52] "Stress, Time & Growth: Factors Affecting Small Business Marketing in 2019." Outbound Engine, March 2019. http://www.outboundengine.com/wp-content/uploads/2019/03/OutboundEngine-Marketing-Survey-2019.pdf.

[53] Doran, G.T. "There's a S.M.A.R.T. Way to Write Management's Goals and Objectives." Management Review (AMA FORUM) 70, no. 11 (1981): 35–36.

[54] Westergaard, Nick. Get Scrappy: Smarter Digital Marketing for Businesses Big and Small. New York: AMACOM, 2016.

[55] Moon, Garrett. "A Survey of 1,597 Marketers Revealed the 4 Steps Behind Every Successful Marketing Strategy." Medium, December 21, 2018. https://medium.com/@garrett_moon/a-survey-of-1-597-marketers-revealed-the-4-steps-behind-every-successful-marketing-strategy-666a0696a5e8.

[56] Beesley, Caron. "How to Set a Marketing Budget That Fits Your Business Goals and Provides a High Return on Investment." U.S. Small Business Administration, June 4, 2012. https://www.sba.gov/taxonomy/term/15051?page=37.

[57] Dallaire, Justin. "Tracing next Steps in Mejuri's Rapid Growth." strategy, May 7, 2019. https://strategyonline.ca/2019/05/07/tracing-next-steps-in-mejuris-rapid-growth/.

[58] Beesley, Caron. "How to Set a Marketing Budget That Fits Your Business Goals and Provides a High Return on Investment." U.S. Small Business Administration, June 4, 2012. https://www.sba.gov/taxonomy/term/15051?page=37.

[59] Ibid.

[60] Brown, David. "5 Ways to Increase Your Jewelry Store's Profit Margin." INSTORE, June 28, 2018. https://instoremag.com/5-ways-to-increase-your-jewelry-store-s-profit-margin/.

[61] "Your Instagram Organic Reach Will Soon Be Zero. Here Are 4 Things You Should Be Doing Now Before It's Gone for Good." Socialinsight.io. Accessed September 13, 2020. https://socialinsight.io/your-instagram-organic-reach-will-soon-be-zero-here-are-4-things-you-should-be-doing-now-before-its-gone-for-good/.

[62] Sopadjieva, Emma, Utpal M Dholakia, and Beth Benjamin. "A Study of 46,000 Shoppers Shows That Omnichannel Retailing Works." Harvard Business Review, January 3, 2017. https://hbr.org/2017/01/a-study-of-46000-shoppers-shows-that-omnichannel-retailing-works.

[63] O'Brien, Mike. "Kendra Scott Quickly Adds Omnichannel Tactics to Address COVID-19." Multichannel Merchant, April 30, 2020. https://multichannelmerchant.com/operations/kendra-scott-quickly-adds-omnichannel-tactics-to-address-covid-19/.

[64] Walk-Morris, Tatiana. "Jewelry Brand Kendra Scott Introduces AR Try-on Tool." Retail Dive, May 5, 2020. https://www.retaildive.com/news/jewelry-brand-kendra-scott-introduces-ar-try-on-tool/577310/.

[65] "Magento Open Source." Magento. Accessed September 13, 2020. https://magento.com/products/magento-open-source.

[66] "Best ECommerce Platform: Flexible Open Source Software for Selling Online." Magento. Accessed September 13, 2020. https://magento.com/advantage.

[67] "WooCommerce Usage Statistics." Built With. Accessed September 13, 2020. https://trends.builtwith.com/shop/WooCommerce.

[68] Rogers, Paul. "Magento Commerce vs Salesforce Commerce Cloud (Demandware)." Paul Rogers, June 18, 2019. https://paulnrogers.com/magento-enterprise-vs-demandware-ecommerce-platform-comparison/.

[69] "Enterprise Ecommerce Platform: Scalable Software & Solutions." Shopify Plus. Accessed September 14, 2020. https://enterprise.plus.shopify.com/growing-your-entire-online-funnel.html.

[70] "57 Shopify Statistics about the Ultimate Ecommerce Solution." HostingTribunal. Accessed September 14, 2020. https://hostingtribunal.com/blog/shopify-statistics/.

[71] Singh, Satyendra. "Impact of Color on Marketing." Management Decision 44, no. 6 (2006): 783–89. https://doi.org/10.1108/00251740610673332.

[72] "Warped Multi-Stone Ring." Cornelia Webb. Accessed September 14, 2020. https://corneliawebb.com/collections/rings/products/warped-multi-stone-ring-sterling-silver-pf20.

[73] Shopify. "Adding Keywords for SEO to Your Shopify Store." Shopify Help Center. Accessed September 14, 2020. https://help.shopify.com/en/manual/promoting-marketing/seo/adding-keywords.

[74] "New Research From De Beers Group Shows US Consumers Will Seek More Meaningful Gifts With Enduring Value After Lockdown." Cision PRNewswire, June 10, 2020. De Beers Group. https://www.prnewswire.com/news-releases/new-research-from-de-

beers-group-shows-us-consumers-will-seek-more-meaningful-gifts-with-enduring-value-after-lockdown-301074001.html.

75 "Double X Crossover Ring with 18K Gold." David Yurman. Accessed September 14, 2020. https://www.davidyurman.com/products/womens/womens-rings/double-x-crossover-ring-with-18k-gold--r07456-s8.pdp.html.

76 "Tiffany Paper Flowers®." Tiffany & Co. Accessed September 14, 2020. https://www.tiffany.com/jewelry/shop/paper-flowers/.

77 Neilsen, Jakob. "How Users Read on the Web." Nielsen Norman Group, September 30, 1997. https://www.nngroup.com/articles/how-users-read-on-the-web/.

78 Lipsman, Andrew, and Cindy Liu. "US Ecommerce 2020." eMarketer, June 8, 2020. https://www.emarketer.com/content/us-ecommerce-2020.

Printed in Great Britain
by Amazon

36234936R00175